T0327815

WEATHER
A-Z

WEATHER
A-Z

The Royal Meteorological Society
in association with Adrienne Le Maistre,
Gavin Pretor-Pinney, Viel Richardson
and LSC Publishing

Published by the Natural History Museum, London

CONTENTS

FOREWORD

I'm not embarrassed to admit it – I'm rather obsessed by the weather. I get excited when I hear snow in the weather forecast and enjoy the thrill of a dramatic thunderstorm. And I know I'm not alone with this obsession. When I meet people and start to talk about the weather, they'll often admit to their own fascination as if it's been a guilty secret for years. The weather is a common topic of discussion, even between strangers. I guess where I may be different, is that I turned my obsession into a career.

However, it's not just a shared interest that we have in the weather but also a shared appreciation of its beauty, its power, its occasional absurdity, its fragility in the face of human activity, and the deep and fundamental influence it has upon us all. Our inquisitive minds asking questions about how, what and why? And the rich vocabulary that opens up when we explore terms originating from other languages, such as 'asperitas' which comes from the Latin word roughness, or 'El Niño' meaning the boy child in Spanish. The weather has a language of its own that has been developed over centuries and now, more than ever, is becoming more relevant to our everyday vocabulary as our climate continues to change. This book explores the weather terms you may have heard but maybe not entirely understood. It explains what the different words mean and through that gives insight into how the weather works.

I'm confident you'll find this book extremely interesting and informative. It is a collection of over 600 words or terms relating to the weather, combined with spectacular images and more detailed special features. I must say a special thank you to Gavin Pretor-Pinney, for his section on 'Cloudspotting for Beginners', which features the clouds that have captured his imagination.

Not only will this book introduce you to a whole new world of weather, you might also find yourself sparking a brand-new conversation about the weather and the impact that our changing climate has on extreme weather events.

Prof Liz Bentley FRMetS
Royal Meteorological Society Chief Executive

▶ *Cloud lightning over West Pier, Brighton, England.*

A

Ablation The disappearance of snow or ice by melting or evaporation. The opposite of accumulation.

Abroholos A violent squall off the coast of Brazil, usually occurring between May and August.

Absolute zero Zero Kelvin (-273.15°C) is the lowest temperature theoretically possible under the laws of thermodynamics. The lowest temperature thought to exist in nature is 3 Kelvin, found deep in outer space.

Acid rain Rain containing relatively high concentrations of acid-forming chemicals, such as sulphuric or nitric acid, that have been released into the atmosphere and combined with water vapour, becoming harmful to the environment.

Accretion The growth of ice particles or snowflakes by collision with supercooled water drops.

Adiabatic process A process which occurs without transferring heat, mass or momentum between a system or air parcel and its surroundings, such as when rising air cools and expands.

Advection The transport of an atmospheric property by the wind.

Advection fog A type of fog formed when warm, moist, stable air moves over a cooler surface. It is most commonly found over cool sea areas in spring and summer, but does occasionally form over land in the winter, especially when the ground is frozen or covered by snow.

Aeronomy The study of regions of the atmosphere more than 20 km (6 miles) from the Earth's surface, which have different fundamental properties to those found in the lower atmosphere.

Aerosol A suspension of fine solid particles or very small liquid droplets in the atmosphere, such as dust or fog.

Aggregation The process of snow or ice crystals colliding with each other, leading to structural growth.

Air The mixture of gases that make up the Earth's atmosphere. The main components of dry air are nitrogen and oxygen, plus small quantities of argon, carbon dioxide, neon, helium, krypton, hydrogen, xenon and ozone.

Air discharge A term used for a flash of lightning from a cloud into the adjacent air, that does not reach the ground. Also known as streak lightning.

Air frost When the air temperature falls below the freezing point of water.

Air mass A large volume of air that has generally uniform temperature and moisture

▼ *Air discharge or streak lightning flashing across the sky over Mersea Island beach, England.*

content. It has distinct boundaries and may extend thousands of kilometres horizontally and usually upwards to near the top of the troposphere.

Albedo The measure of how reflective a surface is. Everything from a desert to a forest will have an albedo value, which impacts directly upon the temperature of the air around it.

Aleutian low Centred near the Aleutian Islands in the north Pacific, this semi-permanent area of low surface pressure is one of the main centres of activity in the atmospheric circulation of the northern hemisphere in the winter.

Alpine glow A beautiful illumination effect seen in mountainous regions around sunset, beginning when the sun is around 2° above the horizon. At its most spectacular, snow-covered mountains in the east assume vivid tones of yellow, pink and purple.

Altimeter An instrument used to measure the altitude of an object above a fixed level.

Altocumulus One of the ten characteristic cloud types (or cloud genera) recognised by the World Meteorological Organization. Its name comes from altum (height) and cumulus (heap). It is usually white or grey and tends to appear as sheets or patches of wavy, rounded masses or rolls.

Altostratus One of the ten characteristic cloud types recognised by the World

Meteorological Organization. Its name comes from altum (height) and stratus (spread out). It appears as a grey-ish or blue-ish sheet of cloud, partly or totally covering the sky, often with parts sufficiently thin to at least vaguely reveal the sun.

Anabatic wind A local wind that blows up a slope heated by sunshine.

Ana front A front at which warm air is moving up the frontal surface to higher altitudes, usually resulting in the main cloud shield and precipitation forming behind the surface frontal boundary. Opposite of kata front.

Anemometer An instrument to measure the speed of the wind. Its name is derived from the Greek word 'anemos', meaning wind.

Aneroid barometer A form of barometer invented by Lucien Vidie in 1843. In its simplest form it consists of a thin, corrugated, hollow disk made from a beryllium and copper alloy. Small changes in external pressure cause the disk to expand or contract.

Antarctic air mass An air mass formed over the cold Antarctic ice cap, which is steadily warmed as it travels across the surrounding oceans.

Anticyclone A weather system with higher pressure in the centre than in its surroundings. An anticyclone is characterized

on a weather chart by completely closed isobars, usually ovoid in form, spreading out from the central high pressure area, and flowing anticlockwise around the centre in the northern hemisphere and clockwise in the southern hemisphere. The presence of an anticyclonic system usually results in dry, settled weather.

Anticyclonic gloom An exception to the fine weather usually associated with anticyclones, anticyclonic gloom results from stratocumulus clouds forming in the moist air below the system, often trapping pollution from towns and cities below.

Anti-trades Anti-trades, also known as countertrades, are winds in the upper atmosphere which blow above and in the opposite direction to the trade winds.

Anthelion A luminous white spot on a faint, curved halo – sometimes called a mock sun – that appears opposite to, and at the same elevation as, the real sun. It is a rare phenomenon, the cause of which remains debated.

Anvil cloud A cloud with a flat, wedge-like top, suggesting the shape of an anvil. Anvil clouds are usually formed from the icy upper portions of cumulonimbus storm clouds. The cloud top is stretched into an anvil shape by strong winds which can lead to the anvil cloud becoming detached from the main cloud.

▶ *Anvil cloud, stretching from the icy top of a cumulonimbus cloud 3 km (2 miles) north of Putnam, Oklahoma, USA.*

AURORA

As children, painting the perfect sky was easy, dipping the paintbrush in one colour without any doubt – after all the sky is blue. When sunlight enters our atmosphere, it is **scattered** in all directions by gases and particles in the air. Blue light has the shortest **wavelength** and is scattered more easily than other colours, and that's why it's the colour we see. Except sometimes it isn't – it is possible to look upwards and see a spectacular display of multicoloured light dancing around the clear night sky. So why is it different? The answer lies in the fact that these lights have been created by gases in the atmosphere, and you've just seen the **aurora** – if you're in the northern hemisphere they're known as aurora borealis, or the Northern Lights, and in the southern hemisphere aurora australis, or the Southern Lights.

It does still all come back to the sun, as a ball of plasma releasing a constant stream of electrically charged particles called the solar wind. This wind moves around the solar system, bumping into planets, including Earth, on its way. Earth is surrounded by a magnetic field, called the magnetosphere, which protects it from the solar wind, essentially stopping the **atmosphere** from being swept away into space. Occasionally, though, there are an increased number of particles – a coronal mass ejection – and the force is enough that when they collide with the magnetosphere they break through, heading down along magnetic field lines, triggering the aurora. Earth's magnetic field lines concentrate toward the magnetic poles, a little offset from our latitudinal poles. Therefore, the aurora will usually be confined to a limited area called the Aurora Belt, a loop centred around the magnetic poles, but roughly sitting between

60° and 70° latitude. But they can occasionally stray further afield, with recorded observations as far away as 50° latitude.

Auroras are a riot of colour, most commonly seen as a pale green or pink light, but they can also be violet, blue, yellow and occasionally orange or white. So why the colour? Well, when

the particles enter our atmosphere, they smash into gas molecules there, breaking them apart. When those molecules come back together again they've got more energy than they need and so release the excess as coloured light. Different gases will emit a different coloured light, with **oxygen** molecules at

▲ *Vivid colours of the aurora borealis, Murmansk region, Russia.*

around 95 km (60 miles) above the Earth's surface responsible for green light, and at 320 km (200 miles) up, red. **Nitrogen** molecules produce blue, violet and red light.

Arctic air mass An air mass formed over the cold Arctic ice cap. If this moves south during winter and spring, Arctic air will bring low temperatures and snow showers to large areas within Europe, North Americas and northern Asia.

Arcus cloud Low-level long clouds often associated with powerful storms or thunderstorms. Roll clouds and shelf clouds are the two most common forms.

Asperitas A supplementary cloud feature characterized by well-defined, wave-like structures in the underside of a cloud, sometimes descending into sharp points. It often has the appearance of a roughened sea surface, as if viewed from below. Asperitas usually occurs in association with stratocumulus and altocumulus clouds.

Atmosphere The envelope of various gases that covers the Earth and is held in place by gravity. The atmosphere is divided into four regions – troposphere, stratosphere, mesosphere, and thermosphere. Atmospheric gases scatter blue light more readily, which is why we see the sky as being blue.

Aurora Taking its name from the Latin for dawn, aurora is the phenomenon of visible light being emitted by the high atmosphere. Caused when charged particles emitted by the sun are deflected by the Earth's permanent magnetic field towards the poles where they interact with the atmosphere to produce light. The terms 'aurora borealis' (or northern lights) and 'aurora australis' (or southern lights) are applied to the occurrence of aurora in the northern and southern hemispheres respectively.

Autumn Meteorologically speaking, the name applied in the northern hemisphere to the months September, October and November, and in the southern hemisphere March, April and May. This season is only really relevant outside of the tropics where four distinct climatic seasons occur. Astronomically, it is the period between the autumn equinox and the winter solstice.

Avalanche wind A wind caused by the descending mass of snow and ice during an avalanche. Avalanche winds can be extremely strong and are capable of causing destruction at some distance from the avalanche.

Azores anticyclone A region of high atmospheric pressure which appears on mean surface-pressure charts over the subtropical region of the Atlantic Ocean surrounding the Azores islands in the northern hemisphere.

B

Backing A counter-clockwise change in wind direction, for example, easterly to north-easterly. The opposite of 'veering'.

Baguio A severe tropical cyclone in the Philippines. Takes its name from the city of Baguio, which was hit by a huge storm in July 1911, receiving 1,168 mm (46 in) of rainfall in 24 hours.

Ball lightning A rare form of lightning consisting of a bright ball of lightning floating through the air. Its existence has been disputed for many years, and though there is now broad agreement that it does exist, its causes are still debated.

Balloon sounding A vertical exploration of the atmosphere using a radiosonde attached to a free-flight balloon filled with a gas lighter than air, usually helium. These balloons are extremely robust and can reach heights of up to 40 km (25 miles).

Banner cloud A stationary orographically formed cloud that extends downwind from an isolated mountain peak. It gets its name from the fact that it looks a little like a banner blowing in the wind.

▼ Banner cloud, taken from the Air Traffic Control tower at Gibraltar Airport.

Baroclinic zone An area in which a temperature gradient exists on a constant pressure surface. Baroclinic zones are characterized by wind shear and are favoured for strengthening and weakening weather systems.

Barometer An instrument for measuring atmospheric pressure.

Barothermograph An instrument for measuring both temperature and pressure at the same time.

Bathythermograph An instrument that records changes in sea temperatures at differing depths. It can be used in a specific column of water or trailed behind a moving vessel.

Beaufort scale An internationally recognised scale representing wind speeds. Units range from 0, which is completely calm, to 12, which is a hurricane. Created by Admiral Francis Beaufort in 1806, initially based on observed sea conditions, it has been refined over the years but remains the most widely used system for classifying wind speed.

Beaufort notation Created by Admiral Francis Beaufort, Beaufort notation is an internationally recognised form of shorthand for recording weather conditions using letters and numbers. For example, 'r' stands for rain and 't' stands for thunder. It was first devised for use at sea, but is equally useful on land.

Berg A wind which blows from inland mountains of South Africa and Namibia towards the coast during winter, creating unseasonally high temperatures.

Bergeron-Findeisen theory A theory, proposed by T Bergeron, and subsequently developed by W Findeisen, that provides the mechanism behind the growth of raindrops in a cloud composed of both ice crystals and liquid water drops.

Billow clouds Parallel rolls of cloud separated by narrow strips of clear sky. The term is the popular name for the undulatus variety of cloud.

Bioclimatology The study of how climate relates to life and health. With the increase in the debate about climate change this field of climatology has seen a rapid growth of interest, studying as it does the effect on populations of different types of climatic conditions.

Biosphere The zone between the Earth and the atmosphere in which it is possible for life to exist in its natural state. It consists of the land surface layer of the Earth's crust, the sea and the lower atmosphere.

Bishop's ring A dull reddish-brown ring which can sometimes be seen around the sun in a clear sky. It is attributed to diffraction which is caused by fine dust in the upper atmosphere. It was first observed by Rev S Bishop of Honolulu during the eruption of Krakatoa in 1883 and remained visible for three years.

Black ice A thin transparent sheet of ice which is dark in colour when on black surfaces, such as tarmac and is the cause of many car accidents in winter. It usually forms when slight rain falls on road surfaces which are below the freezing point of water, but can also be formed by supercooled fog droplets hitting any obstacles such as bridges and trees.

Blizzard Heavy snowfall combined with sustained strong winds, usually at least 56 kmh (35 mph) and lasting for at least 3 hours. It is the strength of the wind that differentiates a blizzard from a snowstorm, reducing the visibility due to blowing or drifting snow.

Blocking A situation in which the normal progress of a seasonal weather system is halted for several days or weeks. Blocking events are generally caused by anticyclones stalling in a specific area and preventing any other weather systems from moving in.

Blood rain This dramatic name is given to a red coloured rain caused by fine dust particles carried into the upper atmosphere by wind currents. These can be carried for long distances before falling as blood rain far from the dust's original home.

Blue moon/sun A phenomenon that occurs when particles such as volcanic ash or smoke in the atmosphere preferentially scatter red light. This makes the moon or sun appear to be

blue or sometimes green in colour, and is extremely rare. Astronomically blue moon is also used to describe the second of two full moons in a calendar month, or the third of four full moons in a single season.

Bolide A meteor large enough to cause an explosion as it is destroyed by the Earth's atmosphere.

Bora A northeasterly wind that blows down from the mountains of the eastern Adriatic. It is cold, usually dry and occasionally violent and, if associated with a depression over the Adriatic, can bring cloud and heavy snow. The term borina is used to denote a weak bora.

Boreal climate A climate which is characterized by having a

▲ *Blizzard conditions in Nikolaevsk-on-Amur, Khabarovsk Territory, Russia.*

wide annual temperature range. The cycle includes a snowy winter and a warm summer and generally occurs in continental regions between the latitudes of 40° and 60° north.

Boundary layer The bottom layer of the troposphere that is in contact with the Earth's surface, affected by friction and often turbulent, it can vary in depth (from tens of metres to several kilometres) depending on the surface type, the stability of the air and the time of day.

Bouguer's halo A ring of light centred on the anti-solar point – a point in the sky at a 180° angle from the sun. The halo tends to be very faint and white in colour, and its presence has been ascribed to ice crystals in the atmosphere.

Boyle's law First published in 1662 by Robert Boyle, the law describes the inversely proportional relationship between the pressure and the volume of a gas in a fixed mass at a constant temperature.

Brave west winds A nautical term for the strong and rather persistent westerly winds over the oceans in temperate latitude. Also known as the roaring forties.

British thermal unit A unit of energy defined as the amount of heat needed to raise the temperature of a pound of water by 1°F, which is equal to 252.1 calories or 1,055 Joules. It has been supplanted by the SI (International System of Units), but it remains in use in many areas of the world.

Brocken spectre The Brocken spectre appears when the low sun is behind an observer who is looking downwards into mist or cloud from a ridge or peak. The spectre – a shadowy figure, standing in the distance – appears to be terrifyingly large, but is simply the shadow of the climber projected forward through the mist.

Brückner cycles The broad cycles of wet and cool periods alternating with warmer and drier periods between the years 1020–1890. The cycles, identified by E Brückner in 1890, ranged from 20 years to 50 years with an average of around 35 years.

Buoyancy The force caused by differences in pressure acting on opposite sides of an object that enables objects to float, or to ascend through and remain freely suspended in the atmosphere.

Buran A strong northeasterly wind in Russia or central Asia, usually occurring in the winter and often causing snowdrifts.

▶ *The Brocken spectre shadow figure of a person in Lochnagar, the Cairngorms, Scotland.*

C

Calm The absence of appreciable wind, classified as zero on the Beaufort scale.

Calvus In Latin, calvus means 'bald' or 'stripped'. In weather-speak, calvus means a Cumulonimbus cloud whose upper structure starts to lose its heaped or fluffy outline. The result is a whitish mass with more or less vertical striations – hence the term 'stripped'.

Capillatus Another species of cumulonimbus cloud. This one is characterized by the presence, mostly in its upper portion, of distinct cirriform parts of clearly striated structure. These fibrous looking parts can take the form of an anvil, a plume, or a vast, untidy mass of hair – which is exactly what the Latin word 'capillatus' actually means.

Carbon dioxide Known also by its chemical formula CO_2, this gas is created by life forms and by burning of carbon compounds, and is used by plants in photosynthesis. A colourless gas and the fourth most abundant gas in dry air, CO_2 is highly soluble, with the oceans providing an important store for Earth's carbon. It is a very strong greenhouse gas and has important radiative effects. The measured amount of carbon dioxide in the atmosphere has increased significantly in recent years – a rise which is playing a major role in global warming.

Castellanus A cloud species that takes its name from the Latin term 'castellum' (meaning castle), so called because the upper part of the cloud takes the form of turrets. The turrets, some of which are taller than they are wide, are connected by a common base and seem to be arranged in lines, giving the clouds a crenelated appearance.

Ceiling The maximum height to which an airborne object – balloon, aircraft, rocket, parcel of air – can rise under a certain set of conditions.

Celestial sphere An imaginary sphere, concentric with the Earth, on the inner surface of which so-called heavenly bodies appear to be lying. It is a practical tool for positional astronomy.

Celsius scale A temperature scale introduced in 1742 by Swedish astronomer Anders Celsius. Based on the division of the interval between water's freezing and boiling points into 100 parts. The system originally devised by Celsius designated the lowest of these points, freezing, as 100. In 1744, the year of Celsius's death, the scale was reversed. The name Celsius stuck, although the alternative names centigrade and centesimal are occasionally used.

Centre of action In 1881 French meteorologist Teisserenc de Bort, famous for his discovery of the stratosphere, introduced this term to refer to semi-permanent pressure systems that regularly appear in one particular area. Well known centres of action include the Aleutian low, the Azores high, and the St Helena high – an area of high pressure located over the western north Atlantic Ocean that can also be taken as a westward extension of the Azores high.

Ceraunometer A radio receiver designed to count and give warning of the occurrence of lightning flashes within a local area.

Chinook A warm, dry, westerly wind on the eastern side of the Rocky Mountains, the arrival of which often results in rapid snow melt.

Cirrocumulus One of the ten characteristic cloud types (or cloud genera) recognised by the World Meteorological Organization. It generally appears high in the sky as a patch of cloudlets that, from the ground, look like tiny wide grains or ripples.

Cirrostratus One of the ten characteristic cloud types (or cloud genera) recognised by the World Meteorological Organization. It consists of a high layer of ice crystals that

▶ *Cirrocumulus over Holy Island, off the Northumberland coast, England.*

appear often as a milky veil across the sky and can produce a halo around the sun or moon.

Cirrus One of the ten characteristic cloud types (or cloud genera) recognised by theWorld Meteorological Organization. Its name is Latin for a lock of hair, perfectly describing its silky white filaments.

Clear air turbulence Turbulence in clear air, observed mainly at high altitude, although it can occur at any level. It is usually caused by convective cloud, marked wind sheer or occasionally by rough ground.

Clear sky A day of clear sky as defined by an International Meeting at Utrecht in 1874 is one on which the average cloudiness during the hours of observation is less than 20% of the sky. In 1949, with the adoption of the okta unit (an area equal to one eighth of the sky), a day of clear sky was redefined to require an average of less than two oktas.

Climagram A diagram used to plot monthly values of meteorological elements to represent the annual variation of the relationship of the elements.

Climate The difference between weather and climate is quite simply one of time. Climate refers to meteorological conditions that characterize a place over a particular period – usually 30 years – and can include information about temperature, precipitation,

wind and the number of days when frost occurs. Weather also refers to these conditions, but at a given time: in other words, the weather on one Thursday in St Lucia may be cold, but the assertion that the Caribbean has a warm climate would still stand. The climate of a locality is mainly governed by factors of latitude, position relative to continents and oceans, position relative to large scale atmospheric circulation, altitude and local geographical features.

Climate change A systematic change in the long term statistics of the climate elements, such as wind, precipitation and temperature, sustained over several decades or longer. Prior to 1850 such changes were seen in fluctuations of Alpine glaciers, variations in the level of Asian salt lakes and variations in the rate of growth of the sequoia trees in California. These days climate change is widely seen as referring to the warming effects caused by the burning of fossil fuels and deforestation on the global climate. The United Nations Framework Convention on Climate Change defines climate change as: 'A change of climate which is attributed directly or indirectly to human activity that alters the composition of the global atmosphere and which is in addition to natural climate variability observed over comparable time periods.'

Climatic optimum That period, lasting from about 5,000 to 2,000 BC, when average temperatures are considered to have reached

their highest level since the last ice age. In Europe, temperatures are thought to have averaged about 2 or 3°C (4 or 5°F) higher than they are at the moment.

Climatic zones Arrangement of wind, rainfall and temperature around the world falls into five main categories: Tropical – found closest to the equator, Dry – including the subtropical steppe

and desert areas, Temperate, Continental and Polar.

Climatology The study of climate. The word climate comes from a Greek word meaning 'to incline', referring to the inclination of sun rays which change with latitude.

Cloud An aggregate of very small water droplets, ice crystals or both, floating in the air with the cloud base above the Earth's surface.

Cloud amount The amount of sky covered by cloud at a given time, measured in oktas – a unit of an eighth of the entire sky. Partial cloud amount refers to a specified cloud type, while total cloud amount refers to coverage by all cloud types.

Cloud base The lowest point in the sky at which clear air or haze perceptibly gives way to water droplets or ice crystals.

Cloudburst A descriptive word for a sudden and very heavy shower, often accompanied by thunder and hail.

▼ *A short, sharp cloud burst along the shores of Mono Lake in Mono County, California, USA.*

Cloud condensation nuclei Very small aerosol particles in the air on which water vapour condenses and forms cloud droplets.

Cloud discharge A lightning flash confined within a thundercloud.

Cloud seeding An attempted modification of the physical processes within natural clouds. The practice of injecting clouds with a 'seeding agent' to stimulate or inhibit precipitation and fog was made famous by the Chinese government in 2008, when it was claimed that cloud seeding had been used to keep rain clouds away from the Beijing Olympics. Common seeding agents include dry ice and silver iodide.

Cloud street An elongated line of cumulus clouds, running parallel to the wind direction. The presence of thermals often gives rise to cloud streets.

Coalescence The merging of two water drops into a single larger drop after collision.

Cold front A boundary between two different air masses, the movement of which means that a colder air mass is replacing a warmer one. Its passage is usually marked by a rise in pressure and a fall in temperature, accompanied by rain.

Concrete minimum temperature The lowest temperature measured by a thermometer freely exposed to the open air and in contact with a horizontal slab of concrete, which is exposed to the open sky and is flush with the surrounding ground. Measurements are mainly relevant to ice formation on roads and runways.

Condensation The formation of liquid water from water vapour typically formed through cooling.

Congestus Meaning piled up in Latin, congestus is a species of cloud consisting of cumulus clouds which bulge out at the top, resembling cauliflowers.

Continental air mass An air mass formed over the interior of a large land mass at mid-latitudes. Main features include a high range of temperatures – with hot summers and cold winters – and relatively low rainfall.

Contrail A common abbreviation for 'condensation trail'– the thin trail of water droplets or ice crystals produced by aircraft engines, also called a vapour trail.

Convection The motion within a fluid caused by a temperature imbalance, leading to mixing of the properties of that fluid.

Convective rain Rainfall caused by vertical motion, usually in cumulonimbus clouds. Convective rain tends to be of greater intensity than the other two forms of rainfall – cyclonic and orographic – and is sometimes accompanied by thunder.

Convergence In a horizontal place convergence indicates that more air is entering an area than leaving it, resulting in vertical motion of the air. The opposite of divergence.

Coriolis effect An apparent deflection of free moving objects, including in oceanic and atmospheric circulation, caused by the rotation of the Earth. It deflects winds to the right in the northern hemisphere and to the left in the southern hemisphere.

Corona A series of coloured rings that appear around the moon or the sun when veiled by thin cloud, produced by diffraction of light by water drops. The coloured rings are blue/violet inside, progressing through to orange/red in the outer rings.

Crachin A period of drizzle with low stratus, fog or mist. Crachin is derived from Norman French, but is also used in parts of Asia, such as between January and April in the China Sea where it may persist for several days.

Crepuscular rays Originally applied to shafts of light radiating upwards in the sky just after the sun has set – the Latin word 'crepusculum' means twilight. It is now also used to describe shadowed bands cast by clouds at any time of the day. Often the beams and shadows appear to radiate from a single point in the sky, streaming through gaps in clouds or between objects such as buildings and trees.

Cumulonimbus One of the ten characteristic cloud types (or cloud genera) recognised by the World Meteorological Organization. Its name comes from 'cumulus' (heap) and 'nimbus' (rainy). It is the largest, densest and darkest of clouds, often producing rain, hail, thunder and lightning.

Cumulus One of the ten characteristic cloud types (or cloud genera) recognised by the World Meteorological Organization. Its name means heap. The white clouds are detached and fluffy, with a dense structure and sharp outline.

Cut-off low A closed upper level low pressure system found in mid-latitudes which has been completely cut off from the main flow. Also known as a cold low or cold pool it may remain stationary for several days.

Cyclogenesis The development or strengthening of cyclonic circulation. Rapid or explosive cyclogenesis is often associated with major winter storms, and maybe referred to as a 'weather bomb' by the media.

Cyclone An atmospheric pressure distribution characterized by a low central pressure relative to the surroundings. A cyclone of middle and high latitudes is called a 'depression'. Tropical cyclones of high intensity are known as 'typhoons', 'hurricanes' or 'cyclones' depending upon where in the world they are located, spinning anticlockwise in the northern hemisphere and clockwise in the southern hemisphere.

Cyclonic rain Rainfall associated with depressions and fronts. One of three broad classes of rain – the others being orographic and convective.

▼ *Ethereal crepuscular rays, streaming out over South Tyrol, Italy.*

CLOUDSPOTTING FOR BEGINNERS

GAVIN PRETOR-PINNEY, FOUNDER OF THE CLOUD APPRECIATION SOCIETY, ON THE CLOUDS THAT CAPTURE HIS IMAGINATION

ALTOCUMULUS

Altocumulus is most typically a layer of individual or conjoined cloud clumps that are known as 'cloudlets'. One of the ten cloud genera, it is the mid-level equivalent of the lower Stratocumulus and higher Cirrocumulus equivalents, forming between 2,000 and 7,000 m (6,500 and 23,000 ft) in mid-latitude regions of the world. Of these three main cloud types, Altocumulus tends to be the most dramatic. Its cloudlets can appear arranged in strikingly regular patterns, like countless buns laid out on a baking tray, and they can extend right across the whole sky. By contrast, the lower Stratocumulus tend to look scrappier, their forms churned up by the interactions of the winds with terrain and thermals, and the higher Cirrocumulus tend not to extend over so much of the sky, their tiny cloudlets arranged across in patches.

Some regular patterns of Altocumulus result from 'convection cells'. Whenever a broad layer of warm, moist air develops beneath a layer that is distinctly cooler, the more buoyant air beneath wants to float upwards. It can't all float up at the same time, since the cooler air needs to sink down to replace it, and so the movement naturally arranges itself into rising pockets of warmer air with regions of sinking cooler air in between. The cloudlets of Altocumulus form where the air rises and the gaps that can separate them appear where it sinks. Of all the cloud genera, Altocumulus make for the best sunrises and sunsets. Lit from beneath by the warm hues of a low sun, its bun-like cloudlets appear for a few glorious moments golden and baked to perfection.

▶ *Altocumulus over New Brighton Lighthouse, Wirral, England.*

Cirrus is one of the ten main cloud types, which are known as the cloud 'genera'. It is the most delicate looking of them all, appearing as translucent streaks that resemble watercolour brush strokes across the blue sky or 'rows and floes of angel hair'.

Cirrus are the highest of the ten cloud genera and, unlike the lower, water-droplet clouds like Cumulus, they consist of tiny ice crystals. As these fall from up at the cruising altitudes of jet aircraft, they can pass through layers of the atmosphere that can differ greatly from each other. It is the changing nature of the air they fall through that gives these clouds their beautifully expressive appearance. The celestial locks appear to thicken here or thin out there as the varying temperatures and moisture contents of the air cause the ice crystals to grow or shrink as they fall. Whether they appear brushed into orderly, straight filaments, or messed up into a wild, chaotic confusion depends on how the winds differ through the crystals' descent. Eventually, however, the ice crystals of Cirrus clouds dissipate away again upon reaching the warmer, drier air below.

Some clouds are the type to demand everyone's attention with torrents of rain and crashing thunder, but not the ethereal Cirrus – they speak in a whisper. Yet their message is worth paying attention to. When the flowing filaments of Cirrus gradually thicken and merge to cover the sky, developing perhaps into the continuous layer of ice crystals called **Cirrostratus**, they are conveying a subtle message about the weather in store. Spreading like this, they are the first signs of an approaching warm front, heralding a cloud progression that can lead, in a few hours, to the thick rain-bearing layer cloud called Nimbostratus, which brings periods

of continuous rain or snow. Perhaps Cirrus are not so much the floes of angel hair as the whiskers of a wise old soul, who'll tell you of the weather in store but speaks in a whisper, which only those who pay attention to the sky will ever hear.

▲ *Finer wisps of Cirrus merge into thicker bands of Cirrostratus over Yateley, Hampshire, England.*

You can think of the Cumulonimbus as the 'King or Queen of Clouds'. It is tallest of the ten main cloud types, extending from perhaps a couple of thousand feet right into the upper reaches of the troposphere, perhaps as high as 15,000 m (50,000 ft). This is the storm cloud, which can produce thunder and lightning as well as hail. Seen from a distance, it tends to spread out at the top in an enormous canopy that is often likened to a blacksmith's anvil because it extends out ahead of the storm.

The 'nimbus' part of its name signifies that this is, by definition, a precipitation cloud. The only other main cloud that is classed as such is the **Nimbostratus**. Though they are both precipitating clouds, Cumulonimbus and Nimbostratus shed their moisture in very different ways. Cumulonimbus produces sudden, heavy and generally short-lived showers. These can be torrential, accompanied by strong, gusty winds, and they tend to be localized. The streaks of rain from a distant Cumulonimbus can appear in just one region on the horizon. Nimbostratus, by contrast, produces moderate precipitation that takes a while to arrive and a while – often, it feels, a long while – to depart. In contrast to the tall, majestic form of the Cumulonimbus, the Nimbostratus is just an endless, featureless, thick wet blanket of cloud, making it the least popular cloud genus.

Not so the royalty of the cloud world. Cumulonimbus clouds are the storms that storm chasers chase, especially when they coordinate together as individual cells in enormous multi-cell and supercell storms. They are mighty expressions of the power that drives our atmosphere.

◀ *Cumulonimbus over Portland, Dorset, England.*

CUMULUS

Close your eyes and think of a cloud. What image comes to mind? I bet it's a Cumulus cloud. This feels like the generic cloud, the one that stands for cloud-kind in general. It is the 'fair-weather cloud', and the most light-hearted of all the cloud forms. The reason Cumulus is a fair-weather cloud is because it often forms as a direct consequence of the sunshine warming the ground. This warmth can cause the air just above the ground to expand slightly and float upwards in invisible currents known as thermals. Whenever air rises, it expands, and when air expands, it cools. The cooling of the rising column of air can cause some of the moisture it carries to change form. The water vapour – the invisible gaseous form of water in which it is bouncing around as individual molecules – can condense into droplets of liquid. These countless, minuscule droplets scatter the sunlight as they are borne on the rising thermals, to appear as the distinctive, brilliant-white mounds of Cumulus clouds.

Named from the Latin for a stack or heap, Cumulus are low, solid-looking clumps with flattish bases typically below 2,000 m (6,500 ft) and heaped, cauliflower tops. They are a common cloud that forms right around the world except in polar regions, where the sun never rises high enough in the sky to produce thermals of any consequence. Cumulus look like they would be the most comfortable clouds to sit on and let your imagination kick back. This fact was not missed by the Italian painters of the Baroque period who rarely depicted a saint or an angel without a comfy Cumulus to perch upon. Cumulus may be common, but how many others can claim to be the sofas of the saints?

▶ Cumulus, near Arromanches-les-Bains, Normandy, France.

32

The fluctus cloud looks like a succession of enormous waves breaking onto an invisible shore. It is known by some as the Kelvin-Helmholtz wave cloud, after two 19th-century pioneers in the study of turbulence, physicists Lord Kelvin (William Thomson) and Hermann von Helmholtz. Rare and fleeting, fluctus is not one of the ten main cloud types but classed as a supplementary feature that can appear on a part of one of the main clouds. As such, it can form at all heights in the troposphere – the lower 17 km (11 miles) or so of our atmosphere (in mid-latitude regions) where weather happens – and it can be thought of as a very specific example of the wavy-looking cloud variety called undulatus.

Waves of rising and dipping air occur throughout our atmosphere, which can be thought of as an ocean – just one that consists of gases rather than liquid. When clouds appear in undulating forms they show these otherwise invisible waves of air. The distinctive breaking-wave tops to the undulations of fluctus are caused by wind shear, when there is a distinct change in windspeed with altitude. When cloud develops at the boundary between a region of colder air below and warmer air above, and when the upper layer is moving more rapidly than the lower one, undulations start to develop along the upper surface of the cloud. If the conditions are just right, the tops of the undulations curl over into a succession of vortices. Such curling Kelvin-Helmholtz waves are found not only in our clouds. They develop deep in the oceans between differing layers of seawater, as well as in the churning clouds on the planets Jupiter and Saturn. Since fluctus clouds in our atmosphere hold their shape for no more than a few moments, they are relatively rare and a really great example is the ultimate prize for a cloudspotter.

◀ *Fluctus, over Long Lawford, Rugby, England.*

The lenticularis is a particularly striking cloud. With smooth edges and a disc-like shape, it can look like a flying saucer or, when it is more elongated, an enormous almond. Occasionally, when a lenticularis cloud forms within air made up of layers with differing moisture contents, it can look like a stack of plates, piled one on top of each other. This is when it is given the name *pile d'assiettes*.

Glider pilots have affection for 'lennies' because of the way they indicate where air is consistently rising and so provide their beloved lift. They are 'orographic' clouds, which means they are formed by the wind lifting to pass over raised terrain such as a mountain range. As the wind rises to pass over the mountains, the airstream expands and cools. Sometimes it can cool enough to shed some of its invisible moisture into droplets or ice crystals, which we see as cloud. Many different clouds form in this way but, for them to look like a flying saucer or a stack of plates, atmospheric conditions need to be stable. This means that the air forced upwards as it passes over the high ground readily sinks back down again beyond, and can even continue to rise and fall in a wave-like path. When the air is particularly stable, only minor undulations in terrain like small hills are enough to set off these invisible waves in the winds high above. Sometimes, a line of shimmering white discs can develop on successive crests of air, like UFOs lining up on a flight path. The classification term 'lenticularis', comes from the Latin for a small disc, which the Romans used to refer to lentils. The formation is known as a cloud species, which means it is a specific form of one of the ten main types. It can appear at all cloud levels but the mid-level examples, known as Altocumulus lenticularis, tend to be most dramatic.

Lenticularis don't drift along in the wind. They remain resolutely fixed in position, hovering downwind of the peak in the strong airstreams that cause them. But so long as the wind speed is steady, the positions of the crests of rising air remain fixed like a standing wave on the surface of a stream as the water

rushes over a rock. Gaze up at a 'lennie' hovering in the lee of a mountain, and you can't help half wondering if some mysterious UFO is taking a rest stop. Hanging silently above crag and dale, the lenticularis comes to remind us that clouds are the vehicles of imagination.

▼ *Lenticularis, British Antarctic Survey Rothera Research Station, Antarctic Peninsula.*

The noctilucent cloud is a fascinating addition to the cloud collection of any budding cloudspotter. You could argue, however, that it shouldn't even feature in a book about the weather. This is because noctilucent clouds form so high in the atmosphere, up at altitudes of around 80 km (50 miles), that they are way beyond the 17 km (11 miles) or so in which our normal 'weather clouds' form. They are also known as 'polar mesospheric clouds' since they reside in the very cold and dry part of our atmosphere called the mesosphere and they form most readily over the polar regions. Noctilucent clouds have an eerie, bluish-white appearance, often exhibiting delicate ripples or billows that can extend across large areas of the sky. Their name comes from the Latin for night shining. At such lofty altitudes, they shine out against the darkening sky well after the sun has dropped below the horizon. The lower weather clouds may have darkened in the shadow of the Earth, but these distant, ghostly clouds are high enough to still catch the sunlight. They are rather mysterious phenomena. How and why noctilucent clouds form is still not completely clear. Though temperatures in the mesosphere can be as low as -125°C (-190°F), this is a region where very little moisture is present. No-one knows for sure how the ice crystals that make up these clouds arise in such a dry, remote part of the atmosphere.

The best time to spot noctilucent clouds is in the summer because this, perhaps surprisingly, is when the mesosphere is coldest. When the troposphere far below is warmer it expands, pushing up the atmosphere above, which serves to cool the region up near the fringes of Space where these clouds form. On clear summer nights, look towards the northern sky (or southern, if you are in the southern hemisphere) in the first few hours after sunset

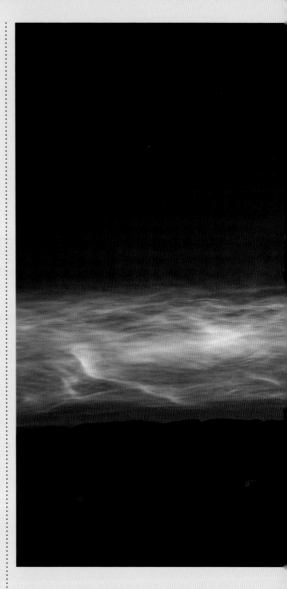

or before sunrise and you may be lucky enough to see some. They tend only to be observed at latitudes higher than 50°, but they seem to be appearing more frequently and extending over lower latitudes, which might be linked to our changing climate.

▲ *Noctilucent cloud, Bolton-le-Sands,*
north west Lancashire, England.

Stratus is one of the layer clouds. It happens to be the lowest of this family of less-than-spectacular looking cloud types, with its base typically no higher than just 500 m (1,600 ft) or so above the surface. The layer cloud family also includes the mid-level **Altostratus** and the high **Cirrostratus** clouds. All of them tend to appear rather featureless from below, and often cover the whole sky, extending sometimes over hundreds of square miles. These layer clouds don't get a great press. As flat expanses of white or grey, they aren't going to win any beauty contests. The lowest of the three, Stratus produces little in the way of precipitation – just an occasional light drizzle or gentle snow – and few would claim that the appearance of this cloud adds a spring to their step. In certain circumstances, however, Stratus can be a truly magical cloud when it forms not in the sky above, but down at ground- or sea-level.

This, of course, is when Stratus goes by the name of fog or mist. As with all cloud formation, the air near the surface has to cool enough for some of its gaseous moisture, or water vapour, to condense into droplets. Ground-level Stratus can form when a gentle breeze of moist air drifts over a cold surface, such as a cold ocean current or an area of thawing snow, or when it delicately stirs the low air as ground temperatures drop throughout a long, cold, starry night. As the warmth of the day picks up, the base of the low layer of cloud can lift so that the boundless blanket of Stratus appears in the sky above – though never far above. Stratus clouds demonstrate in closest proximity the everyday transformation of water from gas to liquid form, turning trees and bushes into ghostly apparitions.

▶ *Stratus near Thonon, close to Lake Geneva and the French Alps.*

D

Dadur The Hindi name given to the local winds in Uttarakhand, India that blow roughly north to south down the Ganges Valley from the Siwalik Hills to the ancient city of Hardwar – a reliable perennial meteorological feature.

Dansgaard-Oeschger events (D-O events) A historic series of rapid climate fluctuations, evidenced by marked changes in Greenland ice cores and characterized by a substantial increase in temperature over a relatively short time (for example, 8°C over 40 years), followed by a cool period, typically lasting a few hundred years. D-O events, which are accompanied by a retreating ice sheet and a rise in sea levels, have been attributed to increases in atmospheric CO_2 and changes in the size of the ice sheets.

Data assimilation The process by which a collection of diverse data, such as surface observations, satellite and radar data, from many locations are brought together to provide a description of the atmosphere at a particular time. This is then the starting point for forecast modelling.

Dawn The first light visible in the sky in the morning before the rising of the sun.

Débâcle The breaking up of ice in rivers at the end of the winter, principally in Russia, Canada and the United States.

Deepening The 'deepening' of a depression means a decrease over time of the pressure at the centre of the system.

Degree A single unit on a scale. On several different temperature scales (Celsius, Kelvin, Fahrenheit), a degree can be defined as a set change in temperature which is a constant. For example, 1°C is 1/100 of the temperature change required to bring water from a frozen state to a gaseous state at normal pressure.

Degree day Calculated from readings of outside air temperature, degree days are used to give an indication of the energy consumption used to heat or cool a building, or the effect on plant growth.

De-icing The process of removing ice, snow or frost from a surface, usually employing both chemical and mechanical methods. Anti-icing is the application of chemicals that not only de-ice but also remain on a surface and continue to delay the re-formation of ice for a period of time, or make mechanical removal of ice easier. De-icing can have serious environmental impacts, with the toxicity of de-icing fluids being of particular concern.

Dendrochronology The science of tree-ring analysis. In many types of wood, scientists can date the formation of a tree ring to the exact calendar year, and analysis of the properties of a ring can provide detailed information about the climate at the time of its formation.

Depression The term applied to a cyclone – an atmospheric pressure distribution characterized by a low central pressure relative to the surroundings – that forms in extratropical latitudes. It is also used to describe weak tropical cyclones.

Derecho Named after the Spanish word for straight, this is a long-lived, widespread, straight-line storm (usually at least 400 km/250 miles long), with winds that assume a bow-shape formation in the upper levels of the troposphere. A derecho tends to occur in summer, when warm air rises over land that is rich in moisture.

Descartes ray A ray of light falling on a sphere of transparent material, such as a water droplet, which after one internal reflection exits the sphere at the smallest possible angle of deviation from the direction of the incident ray; these rays make the primary rainbow.

Desert A large region with little rainfall and sparse vegetation and wildlife.

Desiccation A change in climate – usually a decrease in rainfall – leading to the prolonged disappearance of water from an area.

Dew The condensation of water vapour on an object the temperature of which is colder than the dew point of the surrounding air. Dew forms most easily on exposed surfaces which are not warmed by heat conducted from the ground, such as grass, leaves and railings.

Dewbow A small, ground-level rainbow, caused by the refraction and reflection of sunlight in dewdrops.

Dew point The temperature to which a given parcel of humid air must be cooled, at constant barometric pressure and water vapour content, in order for saturation to occur.

▲ *Dew formed by water vapour condensing on individual grass stems in Lanner, Cornwall, England.*

Dew point depression The difference between the temperature and the dew point temperature at a given height in the atmosphere. The smaller the difference, the greater the amount of moisture present and the higher the relative humidity. The dew point depression is a factor in the formation of tornados, downbursts and microbursts, and also helps in the prediction of wildfires.

Diabatic process A process that sees a temperature change of air not related to its vertical movement, such as by solar radiation heating.

Diamond dust Precipitation that falls from a clear sky in very small ice crystals, often so tiny that they appear to be suspended in the air. Observed especially in clear, calm, cold weather, forming at temperatures typically less than -10°C (14°F).

Diffraction The bending of light waves produced by an obstacle, such as clouds, in its path. Responsible for a number of optical effects in the atmosphere, including corona, bishop's ring and glory.

Diffuse front A front in which changes in air-mass properties, including temperature, humidity and wind, are spread through a wide frontal zone, which can be up to several hundred kilometres in width.

Discharge Also known as St Elmo's fire, a weather phenomenon in which luminous plasma is created by a coronal discharge from a sharp or pointed object in a strong electric field in the atmosphere (such as those generated by thunderstorms or created by a volcanic eruption). St Elmo's fire is named after the patron saint of sailors – the phenomenon sometimes appeared on ships at sea during thunderstorms and was regarded by sailors with religious awe for its glowing ball of light.

Dissipation trail A phenomenon in which an aircraft leaves in its wake a clear passage cut into a cloud. It occurs when the heat released by the aircraft's exhaust is sufficient to counteract the effect of the released water vapour, causing the cloud to evaporate.

Diurnal variation The range of values for a recorded weather element, for example wind or temperature, over the course of 24 hours.

Doister Also spelled 'deaister' or 'dyster', a Scottish name for a severe storm arriving from the sea.

Divergence In a horizontal place divergence indicates that less air is entering an area than leaving it, resulting in vertical motion of the air. The opposite of convergence.

Doldrums The doldrums, also called the 'equatorial calms', are areas of light variable, mainly westerly winds. These shifting, and sometimes completely absent winds, have long been notorious for leaving sailing ships trapped for days.

Downdraft A small scale column of air that moves rapidly towards the ground, often accompanied by precipitation or thunderstorm which may produce damaging surface winds.

Drizzle Very small water droplets, with a diameter between 0.2 and 0.5 mm, which generally fall from low based stratus clouds. High relative humidity is required below the cloud to prevent the tiny drops from evaporating.

Drought A dryness due to absence of rainfall. A meteorological drought refers to a period with significantly less rainfall than the long-term average. The exact length of time and quantity varies from region to region.

Dry season An annually recurring season of a month or more which is marked by an absence of precipitation.

Dusk The last light visible in the sky in the evening after the setting of the sun.

Dust devil (or dust whirl) A whirlwind in a hot, sandy region in which dust and sand are picked up and carried aloft by strong convection.

▶ *The rising swirl of a dust devil forming just south of Uyuni, Bolivia.*

E

Earth thermometer A device for measuring the temperature at a given depth below the ground. It is more commonly called a soil thermometer.

Easterly wave A type of atmospheric trough which moves from east to west across the tropics, bringing cloudy, showery weather.

Ecoclimatology The study of living organisms and their relationship to climate.

Eddy The circular current created around an obstacle when it is hit by a flowing fluid. Eddies in the Earth's bodies of water can range in diameter from millimetres to hundreds of kilometres.

Ekman spiral The rotation caused when the molecules on the surface of a body of water are deflected by the wind, in turn causing the layers of water below to rotate at a rate that diminishes with depth. As a result of the Coriolis effect, the flow is to the right in the northern hemisphere and to the left in the southern. Ekman spirals are also found in the atmosphere.

Electrical storm An alternative name for a thunderstorm, but can also refer to an electric field in the lower atmosphere that comes from dust blown around by strong winds.

Electromagnetic radiation A form of energy that includes infrared, ultraviolet and visible light.

Elephanta A strong south or southeast wind which blows on the Malabar coast of India in September and October, at the end of the southwest monsoon.

Elevation Height above sea level.

El Niño The warming phase of the El Niño Southern Oscillation, characterized by higher than normal sea surface temperatures and lower than normal air surface pressure across the eastern tropical Pacific Ocean.

El Niño Southern Oscillation (ENSO) A periodic, irregular warming and cooling pattern that occurs in the tropical eastern Pacific Ocean, the impact of which can be felt on weather patterns around the world. The warming phase is known as El Niño, the cooling phase as La Niña. Each phase typically happens roughly every two to seven years and lasts for several months, but the same type of event can occur successively or be sustained over several years.

Elvegust A cold descending squall in the upper parts of a Norwegian fjord, also known as 'sno'.

Embata An onshore southwesterly wind caused by the reversal of the northeasterly trade winds in the lee of the Canary Islands.

Ensemble forecast A set of weather forecasts, created by running a computer model multiple times from slightly different starting conditions, giving a range of possible future atmospheric states. The ensemble forecast provides a greater sense of the level of certainty around the resulting prediction and is used by the majority of the world's major meteorological centres.

Entrainment The mixing of environmental air into the updraft of a cumuliform cloud so that the environmental air becomes part of the cloud.

Equatorial air Air that originates as tropical air, enters the equatorial zone and stagnates in the doldrums. Equatorial air becomes moist and unstable.

Equatorial trough The more or less continuous region of low pressure that lies between the subtropical anticyclones close to the equator. This zone is occupied by equatorial air, and over the oceans lies in the belt of the doldrums. In the northern summer over land areas, it often becomes part of the summer monsoon.

Equatorial westerlies Northeast or southeast trade winds that are deflected within the equatorial trough, acquiring a westerly component. This happens when the Intertropical Convergence

Zone – the region over the tropical oceans where the trade winds from the northern and southern hemispheres converge – is located further than 5° from the Equator. The term is also applied to the westerlies that are present throughout most of the year in the eastern Indian Ocean.

Equilux The day on which the length of the day and the night are equal, occurring a few days before the spring equinox and a few days after the autumn equinox.

Equinox The point of intersection of the sun's apparent path and the plane of the Earth's equator, also thought of as the moment of time at which the centre of the visible Sun is directly above the equator. Although the precise date does shift, the spring (or vernal) equinox falls on about 20th March in the northern hemisphere and the autumnal equinox on about 22nd September, with the dates reversed in the southern hemisphere.

Etesian winds Winds with a northerly component that blow between May and September over the Aegean Sea and eastern Mediterranean. Etesian winds are known as 'meltemi' in Turkey.

Evaporation The change of state of liquid water into water vapour. In meteorology it sometimes includes the change of state from solid to gas, although this is more commonly referred to as sublimation.

Evaporation fog A fog formed above a body of water when the relatively warm water evaporates into cool air.

Evapotranspiration The combined processes of evaporation from the Earth's surface and transpiration from plants. The total amount of water transferred from the Earth to the atmosphere.

Exposure A loss of body temperature due to cold atmospheric conditions, properly known as hypothermia. Exposure can occur in weather that is not freezing, as wind, humidity and rain remove body heat. Severe exposure can result in a phenomenon known as 'paradoxical undressing', in which the confused, disorientated sufferer begins to remove their clothes.

Exsiccation Drying by the removal of moisture, often from either draining or increased evaporation. In climatology it implies the loss of moisture without any appreciable change to the average rainfall. Examples include washing away of soil due to deforestation or the advancement of sand dunes over cultivated areas.

Extratropical cyclone A cyclone in the mid or high latitudes that has cold air at its core and fronts attached, and are less powerful than tropical cyclones.

Eye of the storm A roughly circular region of mostly calm weather found at the centre of a strong tropical cyclone. The eye can be 10-50 km (6-31 miles) wide, surrounded by the eyewall.

Eyewall A ring of cumulonimbus cloud that encircles the eye of a tropical cyclone.

EL NIÑO SOUTHERN OSCILLATION (ENSO)

In the early 19th century fishermen in Peru and Ecuador began to refer to the unusually warm waters that reduced their catch around Christmas time as **El Niño**, meaning 'boy child'. Today the term is perhaps the best-known part of one of the most important **climate** phenomena on Earth, the **El Niño Southern Oscillation**, known as ENSO. ENSO is much more than just periods of warmer seas. It is a recurring warming and cooling pattern of change in the temperatures of waters in the central and eastern tropical Pacific Ocean, coupled with changes in the atmosphere that disrupt the pattern of rainfall, wind and pressure in the **tropics**, with global side effects including affecting weather patterns across **mid-latitudes** in the northern hemisphere.

It is a natural phenomenon, cycling over a period between two and seven years, that sees the surface of the tropical Pacific Ocean at times warm or cool between 1°C and 3°C (33.8°F and 37.4°F) compared with the normal. Seen from the South American side, there are three states that make up ENSO: the neutral phase, El Niño which is the warming phase and **La Niña** the cooling phase. While El Niño and La Niña are always followed by a return to the neutral phase, there is no pattern as to whether a warming or cooling event then follows. The outcomes of each event are never exactly the same and are dependent on the intensity of the event and the time of year it occurs.

In the neutral phase, **trade winds** blow east to west across the surface of the tropical Pacific Ocean, bringing warm moist air and warmer surface waters towards the western Pacific, and keeping the central Pacific Ocean relatively cool.

El Niño is the warming phase of the ocean surface, with **rainfall** decreasing over Indonesia and **droughts** likely in eastern Australia, while rainfall increases over the central and eastern tropical Pacific. Low level winds weaken, or in cases with a stronger anomaly, reverse to blow from west to east. This has the effect of slowing the ocean current, allowing warm surface water to build in the eastern ocean. It usually reaches a peak during November to January, before decaying over the next six months.

In contrast, La Niña (meaning 'girl child') is the cooling phase, with easterly equatorial winds strengthening, confining the pool of warmer water to the far western tropical Pacific, increasing rainfall over Indonesia and Australia in winter and spring, and allowing more upwelling of cold, nutrient rich water in the eastern Pacific.

The exact causes of the start of a change aren't fully understood, but a clear link, a **teleconnection**, has been made between ENSO events and the atmospheric **pressure** differences between Darwin, northern Australia and Tahiti in the central South Pacific Ocean. When the pressure difference weakens, it is strongly coincidental with El Niño conditions. Such connections are enabling events to become better modelled, increasing the ability to predict them, and allowing the opportunity to prepare for expected changes in extreme weather events.

▶ The El Niño and La Niña phases of the El Niño Southern Oscillation

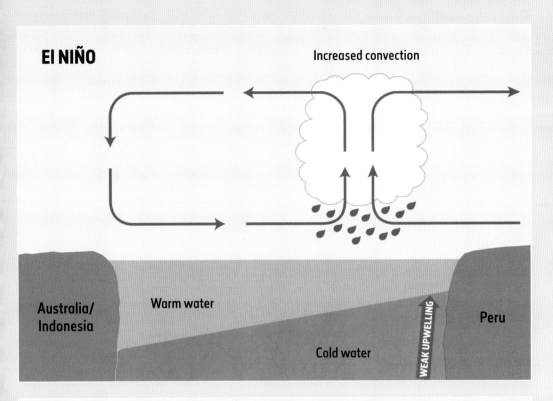

EL NIÑO

Increased convection

Australia/
Indonesia

Warm water

Cold water

WEAK UPWELLING

Peru

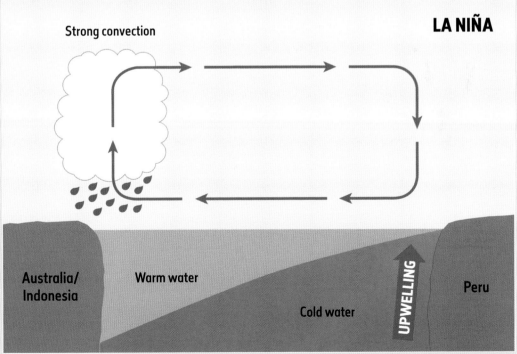

Strong convection

LA NIÑA

Australia/
Indonesia

Warm water

Cold water

UPWELLING

Peru

F

Fahrenheit scale A scale of temperature developed by the German physicist Daniel Gabriel Fahrenheit in the early 18th century. The fixed points were defined as the temperature when a mixture of salt and ice turns to liquid (-17.7°C or 0°F) and the body temperature of a horse (37.3°C or 100°F). It has been superseded by Celsius almost everywhere, except in the USA.

Fair Used to describe relatively benign weather, usually with between 3 and 5 oktas of cloud cover in the sky.

Fallstreak hole Also known as a hole punch cloud, canal cloud or cloud hole. A fallstreak hole is a large circular gap that can appear in cirrocumulus or altocumulus clouds, where temperatures are below zero yet the tiny droplets remain in liquid form – known as supercooled liquids. If they are disturbed (for example by an aeroplane) some water droplets start to freeze, causing other droplets around them to freeze and fall to Earth. This leaves a large hole in the cloud. Occasionally an iridescent rainbow can also be seen in these clouds, due to diffraction of light by the cloud droplets.

Fata Morgana An unusual and complex form of mirage, seen in a narrow band above the horizon, caused by the superposition of several distinct layers of air, each of which refract the light to a differing extent. The name comes from Morgan le Fay, the Arthurian sorceress.

Ferrel cell The name given to the large-scale mid-latitude circulation marked by a sinking motion near 30° and rising motion near 60° latitude.

Fetch The ocean area where waves are generated by winds of nearly constant direction, or the length of that area which will dictate the height of waves formed.

Fibratus A cloud species, from the Latin for fibrous. The term mainly applies to cirrus and cirrostratus clouds.

▼ *Fog, formed by water vapour condensing in the colder air around the hills by Corfe Castle, Dorset, England.*

Fire rainbow A rare and spectacular rainbow-like display, seen smeared across the sky, caused by light passing through wispy, high-altitude cirrus clouds.

Firn A German word for old snow found on top of glaciers, not yet converted into ice. Dense and granular, it is also known as 'névé'.

Floccus A cloud species, from the Latin for 'tuft'. Applies to cirrus, cirrocumulus, altocumulus and stratocumulus clouds.

Fog A suspension of water droplets or ice crystals in the surface layer of the atmosphere, occasionally accompanied by smoke particles, which reduces horizontal visibility to less than 1 km (½ mile). Freezing fog is fog that forms when the air temperature is less than 0°C (32°F), often depositing rime on surfaces.

Fogbow A rainbow visible within fog. Its outer margin has a reddish tint and its inner margin a bluish tint, but the central band is white.

Fog point The air temperature at which fog forms. This temperature varies depending on climate and environment.

▲ *Fogbow, or 'white rainbow', over Glencoe in the Scottish Highlands.*

Fog precipitation Precipitation occasionally caused when low, non-rain-bearing clouds collide with objects such as trees. Also known as 'fog drip'.

Föhn A warm, dry, downslope wind that occurs in the lee (downwind side) of a mountain range and is associated with rapid snow melt. The term originated in the Alps but is now used as a generic term for any mountain range.

Föhn wall A mass of cloud that forms over the windward slope and part of the lee slope, but terminates parallel to the mountain ridge. Associated with Föhn wind.

Forecast A statement of anticipated weather conditions over a specified timeframe, for a particular place or region.

Forked lightning Lightning in which many luminous branches are visible, forking away and downward from the main discharge channel.

Fractus A cloud species, from the Latin for 'broken', characterized by a ragged appearance. Applies to stratus and cumulus clouds.

Frazil ice Loose, randomly oriented, needle-shaped ice, or small plates of ice, which resembles slush and forms in rapidly flowing water, the movement of which prevents the formation of a solid ice sheet.

Freezing level The altitude at which the air temperature first drops below freezing.

▲ *Forked lightning striking the Superstition Mountains east of Phoenix, Arizona, USA.*

Freezing point The temperature at which a substance changes state from liquid to solid. The freezing point of pure water at standard atmospheric pressure is 0°C (32°F).

Freezing rain Rain that falls as a liquid, becomes supercooled close to the ground, and freezes into a glaze on impact with a below freezing temperature surface.

Friction In meteorology, the resistant force of Earth's surface on the motion of the air that flows directly over it, with different surface types affecting the wind direction to varying degrees.

Front A boundary separating two air masses of differing density and, therefore, differing temperature.

Frost A situation in which air temperature is below the freezing point of water. The name is also given to the icy depositions which form on solid surfaces.

Frost day A period of 24 hours during which the minimum temperature is below 0°C (32°F).

Frost heaving The lifting and distortion of a surface caused by freezing water expanding within it. Often results in damage to road surfaces or flower beds.

Frost hollow A valley bottom or a small hollow in which cold air descends and accumulates at night.

Funnel cloud A funnel-shaped cloud of condensed water droplets, associated with a rotating column of wind, that is not in contact with the ground.

Funnelling The process by which a surface wind is forced to blow through a restricted space, such as a valley, and in doing so picks up speed.

▼ *Funnel cloud near Arriba, Colorado, USA.*

G

Gaign A cross-mountain wind in Italy that causes clouds to form on the crests of mountains.

Gale Used loosely in everyday language in phrases such as 'blowing a gale' to describe a very strong wind. In meteorology it is defined as wind speeds of 63-87 kmh (39-54 mph) averaged over a 10 minute period or with gusts of 79 kmh (49 mph) or more, and is equivalent to Force 8 or 9 on the Beaufort Scale.

Gale warning Notification of the likelihood of gales. Terminology used in the British Isles reflects the time of onset of a gale: 'imminent' means gale expected within six hours of time of issue of gale warning; 'soon' means gales within six to 12 hours of time of issue; and 'later' means more than 12 hours from time of issue.

Galileo thermometer Named after Italian physicist Galileo Galilei, it is an instrument made of a sealed glass cylinder containing a clear liquid and a series of objects with different densities, which rise and fall in proportion to their respective density and the density of the surrounding liquid as the temperature changes.

Garbin A southwesterly sea breeze that develops in the southwest of France during the summer months due to the difference between land and sea surface temperatures. In Catalonia the sea breeze is called 'garbi' and the Spanish equivalent is known as the 'garbino'.

Gegenschein A German word meaning counter shine, this is a faint luminous patch of light seen in the night sky at the point in the celestial sphere that is opposite the position of the sun. It forms when sunlight is scattered by particles in interplanetary space and is not visible in most inhabited regions due to light pollution.

General circulation The global atmospheric motions resulting from the temperature and pressure differences due to the greater amount of solar radiation per unit area on the surface at the equator, relative to the poles. The effect of the general circulation is to mix the air between higher and lower latitudes through a three-dimensional circulation.

Genoa low A low pressure area that develops to the south of the Alps in the Gulf of Genoa. Genoa lows usually remain stationary south of the Alps and form to the lee of high ground when strong winds blow across the mountain ridge. The air on the lee side of a mountain undergoes a 'spin up' motion that causes a low to develop at the surface.

Geopotential The potential energy of a unit mass relative to sea level. Or the amount of work required to lift a unit mass from sea level to the height at which the mass is located.

Geostationary satellite A satellite that rotates around the Earth once every 24 hours, effectively remaining over the same spot above the equator, appearing motionless to ground observers.

Geostrophic wind A theoretical wind that explains why, in the northern hemisphere, low pressure systems spin anticlockwise and high pressure systems spin clockwise, and vice versa in the southern hemisphere. In an unbalanced state, the air naturally moves from high to low pressure, due to the pressure gradient force. As soon as the air starts to move, the Coriolis force deflects it to the right in the northern hemisphere, and to the left in the southern hemisphere. As the air continues to move its speed increases, and so does its Coriolis deflection. The deflection increases until the Coriolis and pressure gradient forces are in balance and the air no longer moves from high to low pressure, but instead moves along an isobar, giving the geostrophic wind.

Glacial phase A period during an ice age when ice sheets extend from the polar regions towards the equator with an average extension south of 75°N in the northern hemisphere. The most recent glacial phase peaked around 21,500 years ago.

Glacier wind A wind that develops above a glacier during the day, moving downhill with maximum speeds about 2 m (6 ft) above the ground. It develops because of the low temperatures close to the glacier, relative to the surrounding air.

Glazed frost A coating of clear, smooth ice that forms when rain or drizzle falls on a frozen surface.

Global warming The long-term gradual heating of Earth's climate observed since the pre-industrial period, largely due to human activity and fossil fuel burning, increasing greenhouse gas levels in the atmosphere.

Glory An optical phenomenon which forms when light is backscattered (a combination of diffraction, reflection and refraction) by uniformly sized water droplets to form coloured rings around the shadow of the observer.

Gradient The rate of change of a physical measurement, e.g. the rate of change in temperature with respect to distance across land.

Grass minimum temperature The lowest temperature measured by a thermometer freely exposed to the open air and in contact with short blades of grass on the ground.

Graupel A German word for the soft hail which forms when supercooled water droplets – where the temperature is below freezing but the droplets remain in a liquid form – freeze on contact with snow flakes or ice

▼ *General circulation of Earth's atmosphere, showing the flow of currents around the planet. (Note the ITCZ is in its equinox position.)*

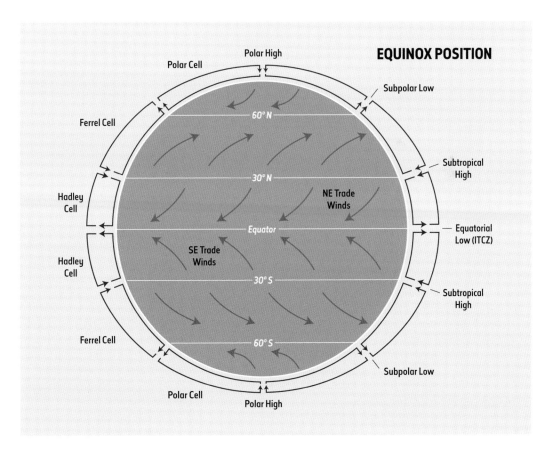

crystals to form small balls of ice about 2–5 mm in diameter.

Gravity wave Gravity waves form in the atmosphere around frontal systems or as the air flows over mountains. They occur when a parcel of air is moved into a region of different density, and the force of gravity pushes it back, resulting in a wave pattern, which will eventually break. They may produce clouds that are visible from the ground.

Green flash Sometimes visible at sunset or sunrise, a brilliant green flash shoots above the horizon, lasting a few seconds. This optical phenomenon occurs as sunlight is refracted by the atmosphere, causing the higher frequency green/blue light to remain visible while the red/orange rays are obstructed by the curvature of the Earth. Green flashes are more likely to be observed in clean air and are enhanced by a mirage–an increase in the density gradient which increases the refraction.

Greenhouse effect Thermal infrared radiation which

▲ Glory seen from an aircraft somewhere above the Hungarian-Slovakian border.

would otherwise leave Earth's atmosphere is absorbed by atmospheric greenhouse gases, such as methane, water vapour and carbon dioxide, causing a significant warming effect. Without greenhouses gases in the Earth's atmosphere, the average temperature of the planet would be 33°C (91°F) cooler than its current temperature of 14°C (57°F). The effect can be either natural or 'enhanced' when it is human induced.

Gregale Strong northeasterly winds which bring cooler conditions to parts of the Mediterranean.

Ground frost When the grass or concrete minimum temperature falls below 0°C (32°F).

Growing season A period of time when the growth of vegetation happens. The length varies by location, and the temperature required varies from around 6°C (42°F) for wheat to 20°C (68°F) for rice.

Gulf stream An ocean current that originates in the Gulf of Mexico and flows up the eastern coast of the United States then eastwards across the Atlantic Ocean at a mean speed of around 6 km (4 miles) per day. It spawns the North Atlantic Drift Current that then runs towards western Europe. Between them they provide a milder climate for the shores they pass, notably Florida and the British Isles, and are the reason, for example, that the British Isles enjoys a warmer climate than Canada, which lies on the same latitude.

Gust A rapid and short-lived increase (at least 19 kmh/ 12 mph) in the wind speed relative to the mean speed.

Gust front The leading edge of cool air rushing down and out from a thunderstorm, creating a line of gusty surface winds, often associated with a marked change in pressure, wind direction or temperature.

▼ *The path of the Gulf Stream and North Atlantic Drift, bringing warmer currents through the Caribbean and across the Atlantic Ocean.*

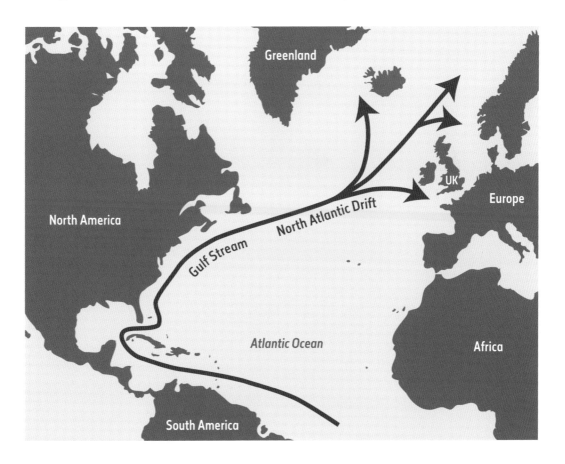

57

GREEN FLASH

Watching a glorious **sunset** is one of life's great pleasures. As the glowing orb descends slowly beneath the horizon, the sky can progress through a kaleidoscope of colour, with oranges, reds, deep blues and violets putting on a show. A few clouds scattered around the evening sky can hugely increase the drama of the moment, as light scattering off their fluffy undersides adds to the spectacle. But every now and then, just as the sun is nearly below the horizon, this familiar spectacle will be interrupted by a dramatic and unexpected interloper: a momentary but very clear flash of bright green light – a small vivid, luminous explosion just above the top of the sun that has no place in your picture-perfect sunset. After a moment of wondering if you saw it at

◀ *A sliver of green momentarily sitting over a 'standard' red, yellow and orange sunset, that defines this green flash, seen looking out towards the Red Sands Forts from Isle of Grain, Kent, England.*

a beach or large lake shore, but occasionally over land, from a mountain top or very high building. The simple explanation of a green flash lies primarily in the fact that our **atmosphere** acts like a prism, refracting light on its journey to the surface, but also partly in **scattering** and absorption. Light moves more slowly in the lower, denser air than in the thinner air above, separating the different colours. Green and blue rays from the upper limb of the setting sun remain visible to the naked eye after the longer-**wavelength** red and orange rays are below the horizon and the yellow rays have been absorbed. Blue light is more readily scattered around on its journey through the **atmosphere** – hence our blue skies – so the light that ultimately ends up reaching us makes the very upper edge of the setting sun look green. This in turn is enhanced by **mirage** effects that distort the green shape we see.

There are four main types of green flash, with the oval flat 'inferior mirage' flash close to sea level the most common, followed by a 'mock mirage' flash which occurs higher in the sky. Rarer are 'subduct' flashes, created when the sun appears to have an hourglass shape, and the rarest being a 'green ray' which shoots up from the sunset point. But it's not just the sun that can create a green flash. The moon and brighter planets like Venus and Jupiter have also generated them, although with nothing like the same brightness.

all, the question becomes, what was it? What you have just seen is called prosaically enough, a 'green flash'. And they're not just confined to sunsets, they can also occur around **sunrise**, and usually last for no more than a second or two.

Green flashes are more likely to be seen in **stable clear air**, when the observer has a clear view of a low horizon usually at sea or from

H

Haar The local name for advection sea fog that affects parts of the east coast of England and Scotland, occurring mainly in spring and early summer.

Haboob The name for a dust or sandstorm. Originating in the northern part of the Sudan where it is most commonly observed between May and September in the afternoon and evening. The name is derived from the Arabian word 'habb' meaning to blow, and the term is now in use elsewhere around the world.

Hadley cell A thermal air circulation comprising of warm air rising near the equator; a high level poleward flow; descending air in the subtropics leading to large scale anticyclones; and a low level flow towards the equator completing the circulation. This conceptual model, first proposed by George Hadley in the 18th century, attempted to explain the trade winds, but Hadley did not take into account the influence of the Earth's rotation, which deflects moving objects sideways.

Hail A form of solid precipitation in the shape of a ball, or clumped together to form irregular shapes, which are often referred to as hailstones.

They can sometimes be as large as a golf ball and on rare occasions can even be the size of a tennis ball. Hail forms inside cumulonimbus clouds with strong updrafts and a high moisture content.

Halo Often associated with saints and angels, in meteorology a halo is a ring of light around the sun or moon produced by the refraction of light by ice crystals suspended inside cirrostratus clouds and can often indicate the approach of a weather front.

Halo phenomena A group of optical phenomena seen around the sun or moon in the form of rings, arcs, pillars and bright spots, produced by the refraction or reflection of light by ice crystals suspended in the atmosphere.

Haze An atmospheric phenomenon where dust, smoke and other particles reduce the visibility. In a surface weather observation, haze is reported when the visibility is more than 1 km (½ mile) and up to 20 km (12 miles).

Heap clouds A term sometimes used to refer to clouds with vertical development, such as cumulus clouds. 'Cumulus' is the Latin word for heap.

Heat low A shallow area of low pressure that develops inland over hot ground during the summer months.

Heatwave A prolonged period of excessively hot weather which

has different definitions around the world relative to the average temperature and weather for a specific location. For example, in Adelaide, Australia a heatwave is defined as five consecutive days at or above 35°C (95°F) or three consecutive days at or above 40°C (104°F); whereas in Denmark a heatwave is a period of three consecutive days where the average temperature across 50% of the country exceeds 28°C (82°F).

Heiligenschein An optical phenomenon producing a ring of bright, white light around a shadow cast on dewy grass where the spherical dew droplets backscatter the light in the direction of the observer.

High Refers to a high-pressure system or anticyclone, where the surface pressure pattern has a central maximum relative to the surroundings. High pressure is usually associated with settled weather.

Hill fog Low cloud which envelops high ground causing a reduction in the visibility. In a surface weather observation this would be to less that 1 km.

Hodograph A graphical interpretation of the wind at different vertical levels represented as a wind vector. Once the wind vectors have been plotted on the hodograph, it is possible to calculate the thermal wind and the position and orientation of warm and cold fronts.

Hoar frost A stunning display of ice crystals that form on surfaces

▼ *A duststorm, also known as a haboob, blowing across Arizona, USA.*

HALO PHENOMENA

On days when high **cirrostratus** clouds are visible in the sky, whether that be ahead of an approaching frontal system or on a benign bright day, it's possible you may see a bizarrely named **sun dog** in the sky. Confusingly not bearing any resemblance to a dog, it can often be seen on the side of a **halo** that circles the sun. While spotting a single halo isn't an uncommon sight, there are other linked optical displays that may be visible to you in the sky, arranged around that halo, making up the group known as halo phenomena. It's a group including rings, arcs, pillars and bright spots, all produced by the **refraction** or **reflection** of sunlight by **ice** crystals suspended in the **atmosphere**. The hexagonal ice crystals, either in the form of

columns or a flatter plate shape, are normally found both in **cirrus** and cirrostratus clouds, but in cold weather they can be found floating near the ground and are known as **diamond dust**. Halo phenomena aren't just confined to daytime; it is possible to see the more common types at night, when the moon provides the light source.

Let's start with the halo that is most frequently seen, the 22° halo to give it its proper name – 22° is roughly the angle between the thumb and little finger of an outstretched splayed hand at arm's length – place your thumb over the sun and the halo will be near the tip of your little finger. Depending on the cloud cover, you may not be able to see a complete circle, but

it shows in the sky as a ring of 22° radius around the sun or moon. It is caused by the double refraction of light through **ice** crystals, passing through sides inclined at 60° to each other. This means most rays are deflected through angles close to 22°, resulting in a circle that is often red on the inside with colours fading or merging to blueish on the outer edge of the circle. The sky within the halo appears dark, as no light is refracted at angles less than 22°.

Less common is the 46° halo – roughly two splayed hands at arm's length, which is always less bright. Formed as light passes through a side face and then an end face of a column-shaped ice crystal, this results in a deflection of at least 46°. However, many rays are deflected through larger angles, so the halo has a more diffuse outer side.

Parhelion, also known as sun dogs or mock suns, are the other most commonly spotted phenomena in the collection. They are spots that are visible close to the 22° halo, and are formed by plate crystals that orientate themselves with their large hexagonal face almost horizontal, with light being deflected by 22°, and visible on a line directly horizontal either side of the sun. They can be very bright, red coloured closest to the sun, or may just be visible as a smudge in the sky.

The parhelic circle is a white horizontal band, in line with the sun, passing through the site of the parhelion. If it's seen in its complete form it stretches all around the sky, but is usually broken into smaller sections. It is formed as sunlight is reflected by vertically aligned plate-shaped ice crystals.

◀ *22° halo, parhelion, light pillars and upper tangent arc near Okehampton, Dartmoor, England. (Also see page 106/107.)*

Light pillars are narrow columns of light seen to extend directly up, and occasionally down, from the sun or the moon. They are the collective reflections from millions of plate-shaped ice crystals that have aligned themselves, and can take on the colour of the light source or the cloud, appearing white or in shades of yellow, red or purple.

Tangent arcs are a collection of several arcs that touch the outside of the 22° and 46° halos and curl away like wings. The upper tangent arc and lower tangent arc touch the 22° halo at its highest and lowest points, but they are often short, or only appear as a bright spot. Infralateral arcs are a rare pair of arcs just outside the 46° halo. They are formed when light passes through two side faces of column-shaped ice crystals that are lying with their long axes horizontally.

A circumzenithal arc is a colourful half circle, around 48° above the sun, and is only seen when the sun is at an elevation of less than 32°. It is caused by the refraction of light through horizontally lying plate-shaped crystals, passing through two sides of it that are lying at 90° to each other. The result is a band with red on the lower side and violet on the upper, looking like an upside-down rainbow, but with the colours much more clearly defined.

And finally, we could see the circumhorizontal arc, an equally bright display seen when the sun is above an elevation of 58°. It manifests itself as a very large, near-horizontal band of colour in the sky, red at the top, with its centre below the sun near the horizon. Although neither a **rainbow** or associated with fire, due to its brightness it has coined itself the alternative name of 'fire rainbow'. This formation relies on plate-shaped crystals, with the light entering through a vertical side and leaving through the lower horizontal surface.

with a temperature below 0°C (32°F) . The initial formation of an ice nucleus leads to further growth of ice crystals by direct deposition of water vapour suspended in the atmosphere that freezes directly onto the ice nucleus. Surfaces become covered with a feathery structure of loose ice crystals which reflect light from all their surfaces and appear white.

Horse latitudes Located between 30–40° north and south of the equator and associated with the subtropical anticyclones where light winds and fine weather conditions dominate.

Humidity A measure of the amount of moisture in the air. In everyday usage it refers to the relative humidity and is expressed as a percentage. Humidity measurements can be used to predict the likelihood of precipitation or fog. In hot climates an increase in humidity reduces the effectiveness of perspiration in cooling the body by reducing the rate of evaporation of moisture from the skin.

Hurricane An intense tropical cyclone – or a warm-core low pressure system – without any identifiable weather fronts, that develops over the tropical or subtropical waters of the Atlantic or Eastern Pacific Oceans, which may be destructive if it moves over land. The Saffir-Simpson Hurricane Scale classifies five hurricane categories.

Hydrogen A gas that is abundant in the universe but occurs in only minute concentrations throughout our atmosphere and is mainly found at high altitudes.

Hydrography The measurement and description of the features of the sea and coastal areas for the primary purpose of navigation and all other marine purposes and activities. It includes the mapping of topographic features under water through the measurement of the depths, tides and currents of oceans. Hydrographical charts include the position and identification of wrecks, reefs, structures, buoys and coastlines.

Hydrology The science of properties of the Earth's water, especially of its movement in relation to the land. It includes the amounts and quality of water moving and accumulating on the land surface and in the soils and rocks near the surface, together with water in rivers, lakes, aquifers and glaciers.

Hygrometer An instrument that measures the water vapour content of the air.

Hygroscope An instrument that visually changes depending on whether the air is dry or moist. A common form of the hygroscope is a 'weather house' with two figures inside that appear through a doorway to inform you of the weather conditions: when the weather is dry the female comes out of the house, while the male comes out when it is damp. A piece of catgut was originally used as the mechanism inside a hygroscope which would twist and untwist in response to the humidity.

I

Ice The solid, crystalline form of water that possesses hexagonal symmetry. When ice melts, it absorbs as much energy as it would take to heat an equivalent mass of water by 80°C (176°F). At the standard atmospheric pressure, ice melts at 0°C (32°F) and during the melting process, the temperature remains constant. Liquid water cooled below 0°C (32°F) usually does not form into ice – it has a tendency to remain supercooled, especially in the absence of ice nuclei, which are very small particles in the atmosphere around which ice can form. Ice is less dense than liquid water, meaning that it floats.

Iceberg A chunk of frozen fresh water created, or 'calved', when the edge of a glacier's ice shelf is exposed to wind, tides and currents sufficiently for a section to break off and float away. The word iceberg comes from the Norweigan 'ijsberg', ijs meaning ice and berg meaning mountain. They are an indicator of climate, and are studied to monitor how cold freshwater melting can influence currents and ocean circulation which themselves can affect weather patterns.

Ice cap A mass of glacial ice that covers less than 50,000 km² of land area. Although not constrained by any particular topographical features, they tend to cover highland areas, with ice flowing away from the highest point towards the ice cap's periphery. They play an important role in creating characteristics of Arctic and Antarctic air masses.

Ice-crystal cloud A cloud, such as cirrus, composed almost exclusively of ice crystals rather than water droplets, giving a fibrous appearance.

Ice day A 24 hour period when the air temperature does not rise above 0°C (32°F).

Icelandic low A semi-permanent centre of low atmospheric pressure located between Iceland and southern Greenland. It plays an important role in the northern hemisphere, forming one part of the north Atlantic oscillation, the other being the Azores high.

Ice pellets A type of solid precipitation that are spherical or irregular in shape, with a diameter of less than 5 mm and usually bounce after hitting the ground. Formed when snowflakes start to melt as they fall from cloud, before refreezing as they reach a cold layer of air close to the Earth's surface.

Ice sheet A mass of glacial ice that covers solid land and is more than 50,000 km (31,000 miles) wide. Also known as a continental glacier, ice sheets currently only exist in Antarctica and Greenland, with the Antarctic sheet covering 14 million km², holding around 90% of the fresh water on the planet. If it melted, sea levels would rise by over 60 m (200 ft).

Ice shelf A permanent floating platform of ice that connects to a landmass. They can be formed by compacted snow which has moved slowly down a slope under the force of its own weight and onto the ocean's surface. Currently only found in Antarctica, Greenland and Canada.

Ice spike An ice formation that protrudes upwards from frozen water. Started by a small imperfection on a body of calm water, as water freezes below the surface the alignment of ice crystals forms a small hole, the volume of ice expands, causing water to be squirted upwards, where it freezes into a spike. It is most frequently found in artificial water containers such as buckets, and is very rarely seen in the natural environment.

Illuminance The measure of the intensity of light striking a surface. It is measured in lux or luminous flux, incident on a surface per unit area.

Illuminometer An instrument used to measure light intensity.

Incus A supplementary cloud feature of the cumulonimbus cloud, commonly known as the thunder cloud. Incus is the Latin word for anvil, and refers to the top of the cloud, which spreads out to form the shape of an anvil.

Indian Ocean Dipole (IOD) Also known as the Indian Niño, an irregular oscillation of sea surface temperatures in which the western Indian Ocean becomes alternatively warmer or colder than the eastern half.

Indian summer A heatwave with above average temperatures occurring in the autumn in the northern hemisphere, especially October and November, following the first damaging frosts of autumn or a period of very cold conditions called the 'squaw winter'. The name 'Indian summer' comes from indigenous peoples of North America who used to depend on a spell of dry sunny weather at this time of year to complete their harvest. The earliest recorded use of the term is from 18th century America.

Infrared radiation A form of electromagnetic radiation, with wavelengths longer than those of visible light but smaller than those of microwave radiation.

Instability A measure of the atmosphere's tendency to encourage vertical motion, instability relates to changes in temperatures with height, known as the lapse rate.

Interglacial phase An interval in which the Earth experiences higher global average temperatures for thousands of years, separating glacial phases within an ice age. Glacial phases are periods of lower global average temperatures. We are currently experiencing

an interglacial phase called the Holocene, which began about 10,000 years ago.

Interpluvial Periods of time with a drier climate during which lakes dry up.

Inversion A temperature increase with height that leads to a stable layer in the atmosphere.

Ionosphere A part of the upper atmosphere above about 50 km (30 miles) in altitude. The ionosphere is characterized by its high concentration of free electrons and ions that are able to reflect radio waves back to the Earth's surface. It is here that the aurora, a display of chromatic lights, occurs.

Intertropical Convergence Zone (ITCZ) A low-latitude zone in which air masses originating in the northern and southern hemispheres converge. Over the oceans, this zone remains relatively fixed, formed by the boundary between the northeasterly and southeasterly trade winds, while over the continents its position varies seasonally.

Iridescent clouds Clouds formed of tiny evenly-sized ice crystals that appear to be randomly tinted with patches of red, green, blue and yellow caused by the diffraction of sun or moonlight by the ice crystals. The word 'iridescent' originates from the Greek word for rainbow. In ancient Greece, the rainbow goddess was called Iris.

Isobar A line of constant atmospheric pressure connecting two points of the same reading at a given time. A chart showing a series of isobars will highlight areas of high and low pressure.

Isohaline A line that connects points of equal salinity. Salinity is the amount of salt dissolved in a solution and is expressed in parts per thousand by weight. As salinity increases, the freezing point of the solution decreases, and the density of the sea water increases.

Isohel A line of constant sunshine duration during a specific time period, 'iso' is a prefix meaning 'equal'.

Isohyet A line of constant rainfall amount for a given time period.

Isotach A line of constant wind speed at a given height in the atmosphere.

Isotherm A line of constant or equal temperature often used on weather maps to divide colour-filled areas which depict how hot or cold it is.

▶ *The random bright colours of iridescent clouds, made up of tiny ice crystals, near Davos, Switzerland.*

J

Jacob's ladder When sunbeams penetrate the gaps in a layer of low cloud they can be rendered luminous by water or dust particles in the air – an effect named after the ladder to heaven dreamt of by the biblical patriarch Jacob.

Jet streak A small area of strong winds in the upper atmosphere, usually less than 100 miles in length, associated with rapidly developing storms at the surface.

Jet stream A narrow, high-altitude belt of wind characterized by strong vertical and lateral wind shears. There are four jet streams circling the globe, two in each hemisphere, and they have a profound influence upon the world's weather. The two polar jet streams are found at about 7–12 km (4–7 miles) above sea level, while the two weaker subtropical jets move more slowly at 10–16 km (6–10 miles) above sea level. Within the hemispheres, however, their path is far from uniform.

Jevons effect The effect of the presence of a rain gauge on measurement of rainfall, discovered in 1871, whereby the gauge creates a disturbance in the airflow around it, such that part of the rain that would normally be captured is carried past the gauge. In modern times rain-gauge shields have been devised to minimize this loss.

▼ *Jacob's Ladder sunbeams climbing up to the skies over Glastonbury Tor, Somerset, England.*

K

Katabatic wind Taking its name from the Greek for 'going downhill', a katabatic wind is produced when cold, dense air flows down slope under the force of gravity.

Kata front A front at which warm air is moving down the frontal surface, usually resulting in the main cloud shield and precipitation forming in front of the surface frontal boundary. Opposite to ana front.

Kelvin effect An effect discovered by Lord Kelvin, who found that the pressure of the vapour above a liquid at equilibrium – known as the vapour pressure – over a curved surface like that of a droplet is greater than the vapour pressure over a flat surface, and that it increases as the radius of the droplet's curvature decreases. In short, the smaller the liquid droplet, the higher the vapour pressure, something which plays an important role in the process of condensation.

Kelvin-Helmholtz instability This arises when there is a strong vertical wind shear across a thin layer in the atmosphere with a marked difference in temperature or density, such as an inversion. The instability leads to spectacular wave-like clouds (called fluctus) that surf across the skyline.

Kew-pattern barometer A portable barometer, originally designed for marine use, named after the Kew Committee of the British Association. Atmospheric pressure acts directly on the surface of the mercury inside, causing the mercury level in the column to rise or fall.

Khamsin A hot, dry, dusty and often rather oppressive southerly or southeasterly wind occurring in north Africa, the eastern Mediterranean and the Arabian Peninsula, but particularly over Egypt. It occurs most frequently between April and June. The same name – which derives from the Arabic for '50', the number of days it's meant to blow for – is also applied to a different wind over the Red Sea.

Knot A wind speed of one nautical mile per hour that equates to approximately 1.15 mph. The unit is widely used in meteorology. It originally derived from counting the number of knots in a line that passed though a sailor's hands in a given time after being cast overboard with a log attached to the end.

Köppen classification A widely used climate classification method, developed by Wladimir Köppen in 1884 to describe the vegetation, temperature, wind and rainfall variations around the world. The main groups include tropical, desert and temperate climates.

Kona storm A seasonal cyclone near the Hawaiian islands, capable of causing considerable damage. Hawaii typically experiences two to three annually, usually between October and April.

Košava An often bitterly cold, squally, south easterly wind which starts in the Carpathian Mountains then follows the Danube through Serbia up as far as Belgrade, and sometimes as far north as Hungary. In the winter it can cause temperatures to drop dramatically.

JET STREAMS

For many it is easy to visualize a river of water, running straight for a while, then buckling as it hits different terrain, before bending back again on its course to the ocean. Look hard enough and you realise that the current in the middle runs faster than closer to the edges. Even if you don't understand all the ins and outs of why a river runs on the course it does, it's an easy process to visualize as a river is physically there, with neatly defined edges. It's no surprise then that it's taken a little longer for the concept of 'rivers of air' high in the atmosphere to be accepted, with the increase in aviation in the first half of the 20th century playing a large part in understanding the science behind what we now know as the jet stream.

A jet stream is a strong flowing ribbon of air, typically a few hundred kilometres wide and less than 5 km (3 miles) deep, that moves around Earth at around the level of the tropopause. It's generally between 9 and 12 km (5.5 and 7.5 miles) above the surface of the Earth near the poles and between 10 and 16 km (6 and 10 miles) above near the equator, often flowing at around 160 kmh (100 mph), but speeds of over 400 kmh (250 mph) have been recorded. The flow isn't always fast enough to be classed as a jet stream so, unlike a river, jet streams may start, stop, split in two, and occasionally flow in the opposite direction to the remainder of the jet.

In the atmosphere air is constantly moving around, spreading heat and energy from the

▼ *The position of the main jet streams found in Earth's atmosphere. (Note that this does not depict the seasonal polar night jets.)*

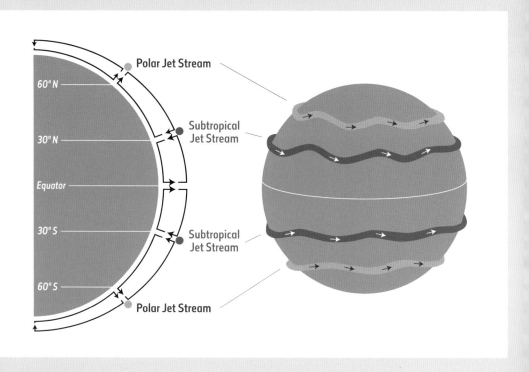

equator to the poles. Within the troposphere, and in each hemisphere, it does this in three large circulation cells – the Polar, the Ferrel and the Hadley cell, which is closest to the equator. Where these cells meet near the tropopause is the place where temperature changes are greatest, and this gradient sets up the faster flow of air. Without any other influences these flows would run uniformly, but land masses such as the Rocky Mountains cause the flow to buckle, and the Coriolis effect accentuates these changes as well as maintaining a general west to east flow in both hemispheres. The large meanders in the jet stream create ridges and troughs known as Rossby waves, but there may also be any number of smaller changes in the flow.

There are two main jet streams in both hemispheres. The strongest are the polar jets, formed where the Polar and Ferrel circulation cells meet, and slightly weaker are the subtropical jets, near the boundary of the Ferrel and Hadley cells. The northern hemisphere polar jet generally flows between 30° and 60° latitude, over North America, Europe, Asia and adjoining oceans, with cold air on its northern side and warm air to the south. The jet stream tends to move south during the winter, when there is a larger temperature difference between the poles and the equator, then move further north in the summer. In the southern hemisphere the polar jet mostly circles Antarctica throughout the year.

So why is the jet stream so important, and why does it have such an influence on the weather on the ground? Well, when winds enter or leave a jet stream they create areas of divergence and convergence, changing the pressure in those spaces. The air below it reacts, either filling the space or taking the excess air away. This effect filters down to the surface, creating areas of high and low pressure. The extent to which these develop are relative to the wavelength of ridges and troughs, as well as the strength of the changes going on above. Usually, the most active weather near the Earth's surface is found ahead of a higher level trough and quieter weather under a higher level ridge - the most rapidly developing depressions nearly always occur below the left exit point of the strongest jets, where the upward rush of air from the surface to fill the void above is strongest. When there is little change in the position of the jet stream, this can allow a series of low pressures to bring wet weather, or extended periods of dry high pressure. Understanding the weather we experience on the ground really does start with understanding the patterns that are going on way above our heads.

The jet stream can, at times, be seen on a loop of satellite pictures, where a fast-moving band of cloud may be easy to spot. And at times, while the jet stream can't be seen, it is something many people will have experienced – many flights will try and make use of the jet stream to cut flight time and save fuel. It explains why flights travelling from east to west, against the jet stream, will often take longer than the reverse journey. But the set-up of the jet stream, with changes in wind speeds over a relatively narrow area, especially where the flow isn't straight, can also lead to bumpy clear air turbulence. This is strongest on the cold side of the jet where changes are more rapid, but the colder air also makes the aircraft's engines operate and burn fuel more efficiently. Severe cases are usually avoided as they may lead to loss of control, but it's not unusual to be asked to buckle up while the pilot navigates through an area of jet stream-created turbulence.

L

Lacunosus A cloud variety, its name derived from the Latin for 'having holes'. Clouds of this variety are thin patches, sheets or layers, marked by round holes, in the style of a net or honeycomb. The term applies mainly to cirrocumulus and altocumulus.

Lag The time between a change in the weather and it being registered by a meteorological instrument.

Lake effect snow Snow showers that are created when cold dry air passes over a large warmer lake and picks up moisture which then falls as snow downwind of the lake.

Lamb daily weather types A method of classifying synoptic weather patterns, providing a perspective on the changing behaviour of atmospheric circulation. Devised in 1972, and based on surface pressure variations around the British Isles, 27 types were identified. It has since been widely used in climatological research in Western Europe.

Land breeze A local wind caused by the difference in diurnal cooling of land and water surfaces. During the night, the land cools quicker than the sea or lake, setting up a breeze that flows offshore from land to water.

La Niña The cooling phase of the El Niño Southern Oscillation, characterized by lower than normal sea surface temperatures and high air surface pressure across the eastern Pacific Ocean.

Lapse rate The rate of change of temperature with height.

Latitude The position of a given point on a north-south plane around the Earth, ranging from 0° at the Equator to 90° north or south at the poles. When combined with the measure of longitude, this coordinate can be used to identify an exact position on the surface of the Earth.

▼ *Lacunosus cloud seen as a thin sheet of altocumulus cloud with a distinctive net like pattern over East Meredith, New York, USA.*

Latent heat Heat that is absorbed or released during a phase change of matter at constant temperature and pressure, such as water melting, freezing or during evaporation.

Layer clouds A general term for flat-looking clouds with no obvious vertical development–as opposed to deeper 'heap clouds' like cumulus. Layer clouds include cirrus and stratus.

Lee depression A non-frontal depression that develops on the lee side of a mountain or raised plateau across the airflow. Common on the southern lee side of the Alps in winter.

Leeward A term meaning 'downwind'. In the case of an easterly wind, anything to the west of a point of reference would be leeward.

Lee waves Waves in the wind flow that form to the lee of high ground, when a layer of stable air covers the top of a hill or mountain and the wind is blowing at least 17 mph. Lee waves may produce clouds along the wave crests with gaps of clear air in between.

Lenticularis A cloud species, its name derived from the Latin for 'lens shaped'. Clouds of this species have an elongated and well-defined outline and are often an explanation for UFO sightings. The term applies mainly to cirrocumulus, altocumulus and stratocumulus.

Leste A hot, dry, southerly wind which occurs around Madeira, the Canary Islands and north Africa.

Levanter A hot, humid easterly or southeasterly wind which blows through the Strait of Gibraltar, usually between June and October. Its impact upon wave and eddy formation in the Straits can make sailing conditions dangerous.

Libeccio A squally westerly or southwesterly wind in the central Mediterranean, which predominates in northern Corsica. It blows all year round but is most common in the winter. Its name comes from the Latin word for 'Libya'.

Lidar Originally a portmanteau of 'light' and 'radar', now an acronym of 'light detection and ranging', lidar is a surveying method that measures the distance to a point illuminated with a pulsed laser light and is capable of detecting particles and varying physical conditions in the atmosphere.

Lifting condensation level The altitude at which a parcel of air becomes saturated when it is lifted adiabatically.

Lightning An electrical discharge associated with a thunderstorm, caused by an unbalanced electric charge either inside a cloud, between a cloud and the adjacent air or between a cloud and the ground. Lightning strikes 40–50 times a second worldwide – close to 1.4 billion per year – with the majority of lightning strikes occurring on land in the tropics. Lightning comes in many different forms, including forked lightning, sheet lightning, ball lightning, chain lightning and pearl necklace lightning.

Liquid water content The measure of the mass of water in a specified volume of dry air. It is a measure that can be particularly useful in predicting the type of cloud that is likely to form in a particular vicinity.

Little Ice Age A period that began in the 16th century and lasted until the late-19th century and was characterized by a period of lower than normal temperatures across the planet, the social, economic and political impacts of which, particularly in Europe, were widely felt.

Logarithmic wind profile A method used to describe the vertical profile of horizontal wind speeds in the lowest 100 m (330 ft) of the atmosphere (the bottom portion of the troposphere).

Longitude The position of a given point on an east-west plane around the Earth, ranging from 0° at the Prime Meridian, which runs through the Royal Observatory in Greenwich, to +180° eastward and −180° westward. When combined with the measure of latitude, this coordinate can be used to identify an exact position on the surface of the Earth.

LIGHTNING

At a church in Devon, England on 21st October 1638, four people reportedly died and approximately 60 were injured when a 2.4 m (nearly 8 ft) ball of fire entered the church, filling it with a foul sulphurous odour and dark, thick smoke. The explanation at the time was that the fireball was 'the devil' or the 'flames of hell'. On 6th August 1944, a ball of fire smashed through a closed window in Uppsala, Sweden, leaving a circular hole about 5 cm (2 in) in diameter. It passed straight through the house and was recorded by a lightning strike tracking system at the Division for Electricity and Lightning Research at Uppsala University. There are many other accounts, ranging in size from a golf ball to a small car, hovering in the air, rolling along the ground or crashing through a window. They last between a few seconds and a couple of minutes before simply disappearing or violently exploding. However, all photographic evidence of them is hotly debated, there is no scientifically confirmed video of it in existence and no-one has been able to replicate a proposed process in a laboratory. This is ball lightning, and it is one of meteorology's most baffling phenomena.

What is better understood is the lightning that we are more used to seeing - that within a **cloud**, between two clouds, and between cloud and air or the ground. There are around 3 million flashes recorded around the world every day, 70% of which are in the **tropics**. Lightning is recorded using both satellite technology and a network of detectors that pick up the radio-frequency pulses emitted. The times at which these pulses reach different sensors can be used to locate the lightning with pin-point accuracy.

Simply put, lightning is a giant spark of electricity in the atmosphere, occurring between

oppositely electrically charged objects. In the early stages of development, air acts as an insulator between the positive and negative charges in the cloud and between the cloud and the ground. When the opposite charges build up enough, this insulating capacity of the air breaks down and there is a rapid discharge of electricity that we know as lightning. The flash of lightning temporarily equalizes the charged regions in the atmosphere until the opposite charges build up again. Lightning comes in many forms and occurs in many situations. It can be seen in volcanic eruptions, extremely intense forest fires, surface nuclear detonations, heavy snowstorms, in large hurricanes and, obviously, in thunderstorms.

Scientists think that the initial process for creating charge regions in **thunderstorms** involves the collision of small **hail** particles with smaller **ice** particles, resulting in electrons being transferred from one to the other and the particles becoming differently charged. Laboratory studies suggest that the smaller ice particles which rise faster in updrafts tend to end up carrying most of the positive charge, and the heavier hail particles (graupel) the negative charge. The result is that the upper part of the thunderstorm cloud becomes positively charged while the middle to lower part becomes negatively charged.

Even though lightning within a single cloud is the most commonly recorded, the best understood form of lightning is that between the cloud and the ground, as that is where it has been easiest to carry out studies and take measurements. Typically, cloud to ground lightning is initiated when a narrow channel of negative charge extends downwards from a

◀ Cloud lightning, with the electrical discharge remaining within the cloud, over West Pier, Brighton, England.

cloud in an invisible 'stepped leader'. As a negative channel approaches the ground a positive streamer reaches up towards it from the nearest highest point on the Earth's surface. When they meet there is briefly a low resistance path, between 2 and 3 cm (0.8 and 1.2 in) wide, between cloud and ground, along which a huge electrical current flows. This heats the air to 30,000°C (54,000 °F) causing a pressure wave, heard as thunder, and a flash of light – our lightning.

Rarely, an electrical discharge can occur above a thunderstorm, appearing as a vertical red column, stretching up to 95 km (60 miles) and usually only seen at night – these are known as 'sprites'. 'Blue jets' are also rarely observed, extending in narrow cones from the top of a cumulonimbus for a fraction of a second. 'Elves' are rapidly expanding disk-shaped glowing regions, up to 480 km (300 miles) in diameter, lasting less than a thousandth of a second, above areas of active cloud to ground lightning, most likely the result of an energetic electromagnetic pulse shooting up into the ionosphere. If there are strong cross winds and many bolts emerging from the cloud, 'ribbon lightning' may occur, as the wind blows each successive return stroke sideways into the previous return stroke.

'Anvil crawlers' or 'rocket lightning' are tree-like discharges, moving along the underside of cumulonimbus anvils, often covering very large distances. 'Sheet lightning' occurs within a single cloud, where the charge runs from the positively charged side to the negatively charged, but the actual bolt is obscured from view and the overall effect is that the whole cloud is illuminated. Lightning comes in many forms, all of them spectacular to see, but when it aims towards Earth's surface it can be destructive and have lethal consequences.

Long-range forecast Weather forecasts made at a range of two weeks or more. Due to the chaotic nature of fluid dynamics governing the jet streams and oceans, long-range forecasts are inevitably less accurate on average than short-range ones.

Looming An optical illusion that occurs when a greater-than-normal rate of decrease of air density with height causes an abnormally large refraction of light. The result is that an object in the distance appears to be higher up than its actual elevation. In some circumstances, this will allow an observer to see an object that would usually be invisible below the horizon.

Low A commonly used term for a region of relatively low pressure, or depression.

Luminosity A measurement of brightness. Or, in more technical terms, the ratio of the luminous flux to the radiant energy flux.

Lumen A measure of the total quantity (and power) of visible light generated by a light source, used as the European Union's standard unit for the brightness of manufactured lights.

▶ *Lightning strike from a thunderstorm over Trail Bay, Australia.*

M

Mackerel sky A sky stippled with rows of small white fluffy clouds (typically cirrocumulus clouds, but also associated with altocumulus clouds) which look like the scales on mackerel.

Madden-Julian Oscillation (MJO) Fluctuations in tropical rainfall, typically recurring every 30 to 60 days, which may influence the timing of global monsoon patterns.

Mamma Smooth, globular pouches that clump together beneath the base of a cumulonimbus cloud, formed by sinking pockets of cold, moist air. They often form on the underside of an anvil cloud – cumulonimbus with a distinctive anvil-top shape – and are usually accompanied by thunderstorms. The name comes from the Latin for breast.

Mares' tails The name given to thin, wispy cirrus clouds (cirrus uncinus) composed of fibrous ice crystals that are blown by strong winds high in the atmosphere and point in the direction of the air movement.

They often appear as strands resembling a horse's tail or 'curly hooks'.

Maritime air mass An air mass that forms over water. It is usually humid, and may be cold or warm.

Maritime climate A climate strongly influenced by the oceans, characterized by cool summers, relative to their latitude, and warm winters. In most cases, it will feature a fairly narrow annual temperature range with few extremes, while

▼ *Mares tails, a form of cirrus cloud, over Starcross, near Exeter, England.*

precipitation is quite evenly spaced over the year.

Maximum temperature thermometer A thermometer used to record the maximum temperature in a given period. The traditional method involves a mercury-in-glass thermometer with a constriction in its neck that prevents the mercury from flowing back as it cools and contracts. Resetting it requires some sharp shaking. The same job can now be done with electronic thermometers that demand no shaking and no poisonous metals.

Maximum-minimum thermometer A thermometer used to record both the maximum and minimum temperatures in a given period. The oldest version, known as Six's thermometer after its 18th century inventor James Six, consists of a U-shaped glass tube, each branch of which measures one of these extremes, with a bulb of alcohol at one end, a vacuum at the other, and a section of mercury around the bend.

Melting level The altitude at which ice crystals and snowflakes begin to melt as they descend through the atmosphere.

Medicanes A portmanteau word that combines 'Mediterranean' with 'hurricanes', used to describe storms with characteristics similar to those of a tropical storm. Medicanes can sometimes form over the Mediterranean region when colder air spreads over the warmer sea, and upper winds are weak.

Meridional flow Large scale atmospheric flow in which the longitudinal component is dominant. Opposite of zonal flow.

Mesocyclone A rapidly rotating column of air, found within a thunderstorm, that often gives rise to a tornado.

Mesoscale weather systems Small scale systems, such as thunderstorms, land-sea breezes and squall lines, which are too small to be shown on a synoptic scale chart.

Mesosphere A part of the atmosphere characterized by decreases in temperature as altitude increases. It is sandwiched between the stratosphere and the thermosphere, from approximately 50 km (31 miles) above the Earth's surface to approximately 85 km (53 miles).

Meteor The visible passage of a meteoroid, comet or asteroid through the upper reaches of the Earth's atmosphere, typically at altitudes of 76-100 km (47-62 miles). Commonly known as a shooting star.

Meteorology The science and study of the physics, chemistry and dynamics of the atmosphere and atmospheric phenomena, and the effects of the atmosphere upon the Earth. A meteorologist is a scientist who studies meteorology. The term was first used by Aristotle in the 4th century BC as the title for a famous treatise.

Methane A chemical compound with the formula CH_4, and an abundant greenhouse gas at higher altitudes. Largely released through the chemical decomposition of organic matter, atmospheric methane has increased by around 150% since the beginning of the industrial revolution. It is feared that with global warming and the melting of permafrost in Siberia, vast amounts of the gas will be released into the atmosphere.

Microburst Short lived convective downdrafts, covering an area less than 4 km (2½ miles) with peak winds lasting 2 to 5 minutes, resulting in strong wind shears than can result in aircraft accidents or property damage.

Microclimate The climate of a small area such as a garden, a location near a body of water, a valley or a city that is distinct from that of the general region. Microclimates can manifest over spatial scales that vary from a few square metres up to several square kilometres.

Mid-latitudes Latitudes of the temperate climate zones, approximately between 30° and 60° north and south of the equator.

◄ *Mamma protruding from the base of a cumulonimbus cloud between Tadcaster and York, England.*

MONSOONS

When we think of visiting some of the great heritage sites in the **tropics** – perhaps the Buddhist temple Angkor Wat in northwest Cambodia – it would seem sensible to avoid the monsoon season. But what is often thought of as the monsoon is, in fact, the summer monsoon rains and is only a part of the annual cycle. The winter monsoon, where dry conditions prevail, is part of the pattern too, and this can be the perfect time to explore these regions. While the most severe rains are usually associated with Southeast Asia, the change between distinct very wet and very dry **seasons** occurs throughout much of the tropics and comes about with a change in the wind direction, blowing from the northeast for half of the year, and southwest for the other. It's this seasonal change in the direction of the strongest winds over a large geographic area that is the true definition of the term monsoon.

Seasonal changes in land temperatures are larger than over oceans. In summer, land will heat up much quicker than water, with air rising over the hotter land mass, resulting in falling **pressure**. The rising air creates rainfall as well as a difference in pressure between land and its surrounding water. This difference causes the wind to flow from the water onto the land – in essence, a giant **sea breeze**, and this is most pronounced and extends furthest inland closest to the equator. In winter, the reverse is true, with the land cooling more readily and the wind flowing from the land out over water. Countries that experience this large seasonal shift in wind direction are known as having a monsoon **climate**.

Such seasonal rainfall isn't confined to land areas - for much of the year there is a band of heavier rainfall that stretches around the globe, with dry regions on either side. We need to look on a large scale for the explanation for this. The **Hadley** cell is one of the three circulation cells found in each hemisphere, and the one closest to the equator. Where the northeasterly **trade winds** of the northern Hadley cell and southeasterly trades of the southern cell come together is called **the Intertropical Convergence Zone (ITCZ),** and it's in this zone that the monsoon rains occur. To either side of the ITCZ, the areas of descending air bring dry conditions.

The ITCZ is where warm humid air rises near the equator, leading to the development of almost perpetual heavy rain and thunderstorms - but it doesn't stay in one place. It moves north and then south during the year, leading to distinct wet and dry seasons in the tropics, and moving the differing direction of trade winds associated with the north and south Hadley cell with it. **Summer** and **winter** see the biggest difference in the heating of the two hemispheres, causing the ITCZ to move further into the northern and southern hemispheres at these times. Coupled with the difference in heating over land and water, the ITCZ will move further north and south over land areas than over water. The result is that in July and August, the ITCZ brings very wet weather to the north of the equator over Africa, Asia and Central America, before moving south into South America, central Africa and Australia by January and February.

▶ *The effect of the land–sea temperature difference in winter and summer in the tropics is the driver for seasonal changes in wind direction.*

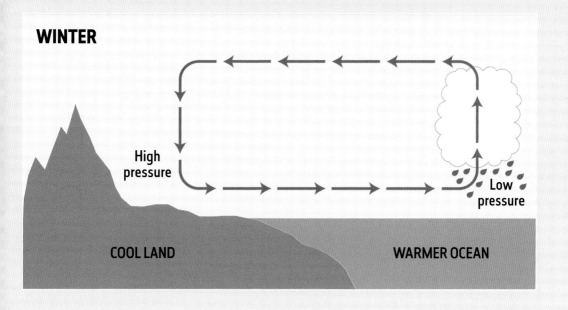

WINTER

High
pressure

Low
pressure

COOL LAND

WARMER OCEAN

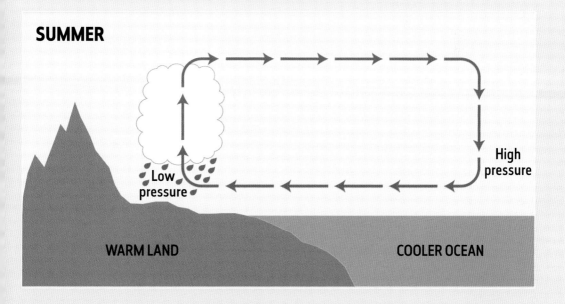

SUMMER

Low
pressure

High
pressure

WARM LAND

COOLER OCEAN

Milankovitch cycle Cyclical changes in the Earth's movements – specifically, orbit (known as 'eccentricity'), axial tilt and rotation ('precession'). In the 1920s, Serbian scientist Milutin Milanković put forward the theory that these variations have a strong influence on climatic patterns.

Millibar A metric unit of pressure, used in weather forecasting. A millibar is one-thousandth of a bar, equivalent to 100,000 Pa.

Mirage An optical illusion caused by the refraction of light through air of differing temperatures, and hence differing densities, causing observers to see displaced images of distant objects or the sky.

Mist The suspension of microscopic water droplets in the atmosphere near the surface, where visibility is greater than 1 km (if visibility is less than 1 km it is defined as fog) and relative humidity is approximately more than 95%.

Mistral A strong, squally, cold, dry wind that blows down the Rhone valley in France, caused by low pressure in the Gulf of Genoa and high pressure in the Bay of Biscay, often lasting for several days.

Mixed precipitation A combination of freezing and frozen precipitation: snow and sleet, snow and freezing rain, or sleet alone. Rain may also be present.

Moisture Water vapour content in the atmosphere, or the total water – liquid, solid or vapour – in a given volume of air.

Monsoon A seasonal shift in wind direction that brings alternate very wet and very dry seasons to the tropics. It is a thermally-driven wind arising from differential heating between a land mass and the adjacent ocean that reverses its direction seasonally.

Morning glory Rare, elongated cloud bands that usually appear in the morning hours, when the atmosphere is relatively stable. Morning glory clouds result from perturbations related to gravitational waves in a stable boundary layer. They are similar to surface water ripples, with several parallel morning glories often seen spreading in the same direction.

Mostly cloudy When between five eighths and seven eighths of the sky is covered by clouds. In meteorological observation this would be classed as 'cloudy'.

Mountain wave Oscillations resulting from the disturbance in the horizontal air flow caused by mountains and ridges. As wind blows up a mountain, downward gusts blow down the lee side.

Muggy A colloquial term for warm and excessively humid conditions.

Multiple-vortex tornado A tornado in which two or more vortices (called sub-vortices or suction vortices) exist at the same time, rotating around a common centre or each other, or inside the main vortex. Multiple-vortex tornadoes can be extremely damaging.

N

Nacreous clouds These are clouds with a vivid iridescent appearance, hence their colloquial name 'mother-of-pearl clouds'. They are formed of small droplets, which scatter light in a way that creates the distinctive luminescent appearance. Nacreous clouds form below -78°C temperatures at altitudes 21,000–30,500 m (68,500–100,000 ft) above the Earth's surface (in the lower stratosphere) over polar regions. They are a form of polar stratospheric cloud.

Natural climate variability Changes to the Earth's climate that occur naturally, without the influence of human activity. These changes, which include both short-term fluctuations and slower, longer-lasting shifts, can be caused by factors such as changes in solar activity, changes in Earth's orbit and axis, changes in ocean circulation, volcanic eruptions, meteor strikes and the El Niño Southern Oscillation.

Navier-Stokes equations A set of coupled differential equations, named after the 19th century physicists Claude-Louis Navier and George Gabriel Stokes, which between them describe how the velocity, pressure, temperature and density of a moving fluid are related.

Neap tide A tide pattern that occurs when the moon is at first or third quarter and the tide-producing effects of the sun and moon are being exerted from opposing directions, partially cancelling each other out. During a neap tide, high tides are lower than average and low tides are higher than the average. Opposite to spring tide.

Near gale A wind that registers 7 on the Beaufort scale – almost, but not quite, gale force. Winds travel at 50–61 kmh (32–38 mph), whole trees can be seen in motion and walking against the wind is an inconvenience.

▼ *Nacreous clouds, formed of ice crystals in the lower stratosphere, over the Lofoten Islands, Norway.*

Nimbostratus clouds One of the ten characteristic cloud types (or cloud genera) recognised by the World Meteorological Organization, named from the Latin for rain and spread out. A low-level, layered cloud usually found below (2,438 m) 8,000 ft, which is uniformly grey in appearance. It is capable of producing rain and/or snow, which often falls continuously and is slight to moderate in intensity.

Nitrogen The chemical element (with the symbol N) that makes up approximately 78% of the volume of the Earth's atmosphere and ranks sixth in cosmic abundance. In its stable, atmospheric form it is a diatomic gas, N_2 – a molecule with two atoms of nitrogen. Nitrogen occurs in all living organisms.

Nitrogen dioxide A chemical compound with the formula NO_2, nitrogen dioxide occurs naturally as a trace gas in the Earth's atmosphere, but it is also a major pollutant created mainly as a waste product from car engines. It is known to contribute to the formation of photochemical smog, which can have significant impacts on human health.

Nitrous oxide A chemical compound with the formula N_2O, emitted mainly as a by-product of burning fossil fuels and agricultural fertilisation, it plays a significant role in the depletion of the ozone layer and is a powerful greenhouse gas.

Noctilucent clouds From the Latin 'night shining', these are clouds found high in the atmosphere, in the layer known as the mesosphere, around 76,000–85,000 m (250,000–280,000 ft) above the Earth's surface. They are thin, bluish-white clouds made up of small ice-particles and are usually too faint to be seen. They most often appear on mid-summer nights (around twilight) between the latitude of 50° and 70°. Also known as polar mesospheric clouds.

Nocturnal Occurring at night-time.

Nocturnal jet A localized, fastmoving air current that occurs in the lower atmosphere during the night.

Nor'easter A strong, low pressure system occurring off the east coast of North America during winter. It can form over land or coastal waters and often produces heavy snow, rain and waves. Wind gusts can exceed hurricane force speeds. It gets its name from the direction of the strong northeasterly winds that blow in from the ocean ahead of the storm.

North Atlantic Oscillation (NAO) A large-scale fluctuation in atmospheric pressure between the subtropical, high pressure system located near the Azores in the Atlantic Ocean and the sub-polar, low pressure system near Iceland. It is quantified in the NAO Index.

NAO index A measure of anomalies in sea level pressure between the Azores high pressure system and the Icelandic low pressure system. When the NAO is in its positive phase (+NAO), the northeastern United States sees an increase in temperature and a decrease in snow days, the central United States has increased precipitation, the North Sea has an increase in storms, and northern Europe has higher temperatures and increased precipitation. When the NAO is in its negative phase (-NAO), the tropical Atlantic and Gulf coast have an increased number of strong hurricanes, northern Europe is drier, and Turkey and other Mediterranean countries have increased precipitation.

Novaya Zemlya effect A rare and complex polar mirage, caused by the refraction of sunlight.

Northern lights Common name for aurora borealis (see Aurora).

Nowcast A very short-term weather forecast, usually for the next six hours or so.

Numerical weather prediction A computer-generated forecast or prediction based on fundamental equations governing the motions and forces affecting the atmosphere and oceans. The computer 'model' is initialized with weather conditions for a specific place and time. Data assimilation is the process by which the optimal initial conditions for numerical forecasts are defined, drawing on real time observations.

O

Observation The source of the fundamental data used in weather forecasting and meteorology. These observations measure quantities such as temperature, humidity, precipitation, air pressure, wind speed and wind direction at a specific location at a specific time.

Observational network An array or group of meteorological observing stations spread over a given area which are used for a specific purpose.

Occluded front The merging of two fronts, as when a cold front catches up to a warm front. The front develops during the later stage of the life cycle of a frontal depression. Two types of occlusion can form: a cold occlusion results when the cold air is behind the front and a warm occlusion results when the cold air is ahead of the front.

Offshore breeze A wind that blows from the land towards a body of water. Also known as a land breeze.

Okta A measurement of total cloud cover. One okta of cloud cover is the equivalent of one eighth of the sky covered with cloud.

Optical phenomenon Atmospheric events caused by the interaction of light and matter, resulting in a visible effect. Examples include rainbows, mirages, green flashes and halos.

Orographic rain Precipitation caused by hills or mountain ranges deflecting moisture-laden air masses upward, forcing the air to cool and the moisture to condense and form orographic clouds and precipitation. One of three broad classes of rain – the others being cyclonic and convective.

Oroshi The Japanese term for a katabatic wind that blows down the slope of a mountain.

Overcast When a full eight eighths of the sky is covered by cloud, leading to grey and dull skies.

Oxygen A chemical element with the symbol O, which comprises approximately 20.8% of the volume of the Earth's atmosphere and is essential to cellular respiration and all organic life forms. Oxygen is replenished on the planet by vegetation through the process of photosynthesis. Marine environments produce around 70% of all the free oxygen in the Earth's atmosphere, while on land, the rainforests in the Congo and the Amazon are important producers.

Ozone A highly reactive gas containing three atoms of oxygen, with the chemical symbol O_3 that occurs naturally in the stratosphere and lower troposphere, in quantities of between 3 and 8 parts per million, but may also be man-made. In the stratosphere it absorbs ultraviolet rays. Close to the ground when released as a pollutant from industrial activity it can contribute to respiratory illness.

Ozone hole A severe depletion of stratospheric ozone (O_3) over Antarctica that occurs each spring. This depletion is caused by a chemical reaction involving ozone and chlorine, primarily from human produced sources.

Ozone layer A layer in the stratosphere (11,000 to 49,000 m/32,000 to 164,000 ft above the Earth's surface) that contains a high concentration of ozone and absorbs most of the sun's ultraviolet (UV) radiation.

NOVAYA ZEMLYA EFFECT

Ancient civilizations, most notably the Babylonians, discovered basic patterns in the movement of the sun and the moon. Many other cultures have since built on this, such that the ability to accurately predict the movement of stars, planets, eclipses and comets has been a science for centuries. We can confidently say what our ever-shifting skies looked like thousands of years ago, and we know what they will look like to our descendants thousands of years in the future. Astronomical predictions provided the very foundations of sea-borne navigation. In the absence of any landmarks, mariners and explorers looked to the heavens to find their way around the Earth, and understanding the patterns could be the difference between life and death. So just imagine the thoughts of Dutch explorer Gerrit de Veer one January morning in 1597 as the sun came up. First of all, it was a very odd shape, but that first slightly flattened disc was followed by another and then another until the sun looked like several fat pancakes stacked on top of each other. The vision persisted even after the sun had cleared the horizon. But the thing that would have really grabbed De Veer's attention was that the sun was early, in fact nearly two weeks early for his location, suggesting he was nowhere near where he thought he was. What Gerrit de Veer had just witnessed was the first recorded sighting of the Novaya Zemlya effect – named after the Arctic archipelago over which that strange sun rose.

It is a particularly rare and complex kind of polar **mirage**, caused by a large **refraction** of sunlight because of the atmospheric thermoclines. An atmospheric thermocline is a thin layer of air in which temperature and density change much more rapidly with height than in the surrounding air. This in turn affects the way light interacts with this layer of air. For the Novaya Zemlya effect to occur, a thermocline has to be sitting at exactly the right altitude at **sunrise** or **sunset**, and this layer has to be warmer than the air below, with the sunlight travelling within it for at least 400 km (250 miles). It is this combination of effects that causes an elevation of the sun's rays by about 5°, causing it to 'rise' early, or indeed 'set' late. The general weather conditions at the time will determine precisely what this early or late sun will look like, but it will always take on a flattened shape. However, because it is possible for several atmospheric thermoclines to exist at different heights at the same time, the light can be bent by several of these layers at once, causing the stacked pancake effect known as a 'rectangular sun'. Whilst the effect is largely seen near the poles, rare sightings have been recorded elsewhere, including in California, USA.

▲ *Novaya Zemlya effect seen from San Francisco, California, USA. The refraction here was small, and the pictures taken after sunset – the top left image just over a minute later, with the series lasting to just over 4 minutes after the sun had sunk below the horizon.*

P

Pacific Decadal Oscillation (PDO) A pattern of climatic variability on a timescale of decades. It is characterized by positive (warm) or negative (cool) sea surface temperature anomalies in the northeast and tropical Pacific Ocean. It primarily affects weather patterns and sea surface temperatures in the Pacific northwest, Alaska, and northern Pacific Islands.

Pancake ice Circular flat disks of ice with a raised edge around the rim caused by repeated collisions with other ice or from the ocean waves.

Parhelion Two bright spots that appear at the same elevation either side of the sun at roughly 22°, creating the illusion of three suns in the sky. They are caused by the refraction of sunlight passing through ice crystals and are most common during mid-latitude winters. They are also known as mock suns or sun dogs.

Partly cloudy When between three eighths and five eighths of the sky is covered by clouds. In meteorological observation this would be classed as 'fair'.

Pascal The unit of pressure, used in aviation meteorology, produced when one newton acts on one square metre (1 N/m^2). It is abbreviated to Pa.

Permafrost A soil layer at varying depths below the surface of tundra regions, that has remained permanently frozen from at least two to several thousand years.

Petrichor A combination of odours from decomposing plant and animal matter attached to rocks or soil that are released when disturbed by raindrops. The odours are stronger after a dry spell. The word originates from the Greek 'petros', meaning stone, and 'ichor', the fluid that flowed through the veins of the gods in ancient Greek mythology.

Phase change The change in matter from one state to another, such as solid to liquid (melting) or gas to liquid (condensation).

Phenology The study of times of naturally occurring events, such as the first blossom appearance in a long-established species, or the departure of migratory birds. Studying phenology can provide an insight into changing seasons.

Photochemical smog Air pollution containing ozone and other reactive chemical compounds, formed by the reaction of nitrogen oxides and hydrocarbons in the presence of sunlight.

Pileus cloud Also known as cap cloud or scarf cloud, this is a small, horizontal cloud that forms above a cumulus or cumulonimbus cloud and looks like a cap made up of ice crystals. They form when strong updrafts occur in a convective cloud and push a dome-shaped air parcel up above the cloud. The moisture in the dome condenses quickly. Pilei can also form over ash clouds and pyro-cumulus clouds.

Pluvial Anything that is brought about directly by precipitation – for example, pluvial flooding is surface flooding caused by heavy rainfall.

Polar air A mass of very cold, dry air that forms in polar regions.

Polar cell The smallest and weakest of the global atmospheric circulations, they are found between 60° and 70° north and south. Air sinks over higher latitudes and flows out at the surface at lower latitudes.

Polar front A boundary that separates tropical air masses from polar air masses.

Polar low Formed in winter, a small intense cyclone formed in cold polar air as it moves over warmer water.

Polar maritime air mass An air mass with its origins in Canada or Greenland, characterized by cold, moist air. Its passage over the relatively warm waters of the North Atlantic sees its temperature rise rapidly and the air becomes very unstable producing many showers.

Polar jet stream A belt of powerful upper-level winds that sits above the polar front, between polar air and subtropical air. It is associated with the location and motion of high and low pressure systems in the mid-latitudes and, therefore, influences weather patterns. Its position tends to migrate south in the Northern Hemispheric winter and north in the summer. Also called a mid-latitude jet stream.

Polar mesospheric clouds Another name for noctilucent clouds.

Polar night jet A core of strong westerly winds formed around 60° latitude in each hemisphere during the longer nights of autumn and winter in the upper stratosphere.

Polar orbiting satellite A weather satellite that travels over both poles each time it orbits the Earth, about 850 km (530 miles) above the Earth's surface.

Polar stratospheric clouds High altitude clouds that form in the stratosphere above polar regions in the extreme cold of winter. Some forms made up of small, supercooled water droplets and nitric acid are known to play a role in the Antarctic ozone hole by providing a surface for chemical reactions that produce an ozone destroying form of chlorine to occur.

▲ *Pileus cloud forming an ice cap over a large cumulus cloud just west of Prague Airport in the Czech Republic.*

Polar vortex A large area of low pressure and cold air generally located above each of the poles high up in the stratosphere which strengthens in the winter, and weakens in the summer.

Pollutant Particles, gases or liquid aerosols in the atmosphere that have an undesirable effect on human health or the environment. In certain conditions, a build-up of air pollution can result in smog.

Potential temperature The temperature a parcel of dry

▲ *Polar stratospheric clouds can be seen in a range of colours, sometimes appearing as a thin yellowish veil. A brighter example is seen here over Alloa, Scotland.*

air would have if it were lifted adiabatically (meaning without transfer of heat or mass) to a standard pressure level.

Powder snow Dry, loose, uncompacted snow.

Precipitation The general term for water falling from clouds to the Earth as a liquid or a solid, including rain, drizzle, freezing rain, hail, sleet and snow.

Pressure The force exerted on an area by the weight of the atmosphere. Units include atmospheres (atm), millibars (mb), Pascals (Pa) and inches of mercury (in).

Pressure gradient force A three-dimensional force that accelerates air parcels from areas of high pressure to areas of low pressure.

Pressure tendency The amount of pressure change at any one location during a specific period of time, usually observed in three-hour intervals. Recorded as pressure rising, pressure falling or pressure steady.

Prevailing wind The most frequent wind direction for any location over a given period, for example, a day, month, season, year or climatological period.

Probability forecast A forecast of the probability that one or more specific weather conditions will occur – for example, a 70% chance of rainfall.

Psychrometer An instrument used to measure the water vapour content of the atmosphere. It consists of two thermometers, a wet bulb and a dry bulb. The cooling that results from evaporation on the wet bulb makes it register a lower temperature than the dry bulb. The difference between the readings provides a measure of the dryness of the atmosphere. Different designs include the 'sling' or 'whirling' psychrometer.

Punch hole cloud Also known as 'fallstreak' or 'holepunch' (see fallstreak hole).

Q

Quasi-Biennial Oscillation (QBO) A periodic oscillation in the direction of tropical lower stratospheric winds, either easterly or westerly. The direction changes every 26 months.

Quasi-stationary front A front which is almost stationary or moves very little. It is also known as a stationary front.

R

Radar Short for 'radio detection and ranging', radar is an instrument that, among many other uses, can be utilized to detect precipitation by measuring the strength of the electromagnetic signal reflected back.

Radiance A measure of the intensity of the radiant energy flux emitted by a body in a given direction.

Radiation Energy transmitted in the form of electromagnetic waves. Radiation has differing characteristics, depending upon the wavelength. Radiation from the sun has a short wavelength (ultra-violet), while energy re-radiated from the Earth's surface and the atmosphere has a long wavelength (infra-red).

Radiation fog Fog that forms over land by the cooling of the near-surface air to below its dew point as it comes into contact with the ground. Also known as ground fog.

Radiometer A device for measuring the power of electromagnetic radiation, such as an ultraviolet (UV) sensor.

Radiosonde An instrument that measures the temperature, pressure and humidity of the atmosphere as it is carried aloft on a balloon. The 'sonde' (a small radio transmitter) sends its measurements to a ground-based radio receiver via radio signals.

Rain / rainfall Liquid precipitation consisting of droplets of water more than 0.5 mm in diameter that fall to the Earth from clouds in the sky.

Rain gauge An instrument used to measure rainfall amounts.

Rain shadow An area on the lee side of a mountain barrier that experiences reduced precipitation due to the warming of air and dissipation of clouds as air descends the barrier.

Rainbow A phenomenon that occurs when sunlight shines through water droplets in the air, during or immediately after a rain shower. The bow is observed in the opposite side of the sky from the sun. The light is refracted when it enters a water droplet, then reflected off the back of the droplet, then dispersed as it leaves. The seven different colours that make up white light (red, orange, yellow, green, blue, indigo, violet) bend by different amounts, so they split and become visible in the shape of an arc, with red on the outer rim, and blue on the inner edge.

Reflection The process whereby radiation (or other wave form) hitting a surface is directed back into the medium through which it travelled.

RAINBOWS

On days when you spot a dark **cloud** on the horizon, creeping closer with ominous signs of **rain** falling from its base, there are times when nature can distract you from thoughts of an impending soaking by delivering a perfect colourful arc in the sky – a rainbow.

A rainbow is a group of concentric arcs with colours ranging across the spectrum from violet to red, produced on a 'screen' of water drops in the **atmosphere** by light from the sun or the moon. Those water drops are usually raindrops from shower clouds, but could be spray from a waterfall or a fountain, or even those in fog. The conditions for all are the same – the observer must have their back to the light source and the water droplets must be in front.

Sunlight is made up of a spectrum of different colours that will slow down and change direction when entering water. This is known as **refraction** - each colour with its different wavelength will bend at slightly different angles so that the light splits into its different component colours. If the angle is right, some of that light will be **reflected** off the internal surface of the raindrop, exiting the drop and refracting again, so that ultimately we see the rainbow with the red band on the outside. Every observer will see a slightly different angle of refraction, so each rainbow is unique to each that person.

How much we see of the arc depends on where we are and how high the sun is in the sky. When the sun is higher in the sky we may see a shallow arc close to the horizon, but being nearer **sunrise** or **sunset** gives the best chance of seeing a full tall semi-circle. And from a plane, the top of a mountain or with a hose in your garden, it is possible to see a full circle.

If you're lucky, there are times you can see two for the price of one. There may still be no

pot of gold, but a double rainbow can be doubly rewarding, and they're not that uncommon if you know to look for them. The second bow appears around 10° above the primary bow, but fainter and nearly twice as wide. They are formed when light is reflected twice within a raindrop, resulting in a second arc with the colour order reversed. The band between the two arcs, known as Alexander's band (after Alexander of Aphrodisias who described it in 200 AD) is dark, as the light is being bent away from the observer.

A moonbow is as straightforward as it sounds, created in the same way as a rainbow but from the weaker light of the moon, so the colours, if seen at all, are very diffuse. To the naked eye they often appear to be white, but the range of colours can be captured on long exposure photographs.

A fogbow, or 'white rainbow', is a similar size but broader than a rainbow. They can be seen by an observer, still with sunlight behind them, looking at a thin fog or mist bank. Sunlight must pass through much smaller water

▲ *Double rainbow seen outside Burlington, on the Kansas–Colorado border, USA.*

droplets, less than 1mm in diameter, that make up the fog or mist. In these much smaller droplets diffraction, rather than refraction, becomes the dominant process. Diffraction is much less wavelength dependent and so the resulting bow appears white, although occasionally the inner and outer edges show faint red and blue tinges.

▲ *Roll cloud, detached from the base of a cumulonimbus cloud, marking the gust front approaching Capo d'Otranto lighthouse, Otranto, Lecce, Italy.*

Reflectivity A measure of how much reflection is occurring.

Refraction Changes in the direction of a light or sound wave when it moves from one medium to another of different density.

Relative humidity The amount of water vapour in the air, expressed as a percentage of the amount that is needed to saturate the air, which varies with temperature.

Ribbon lightning A succession of lightning strikes, each of which is blown to the side of the previous strike by wind, but at such a speed that all the strokes are seen at once as a ribbon-like flash.

Ridge An elongated area of relatively high atmospheric pressure, usually stretching out from the centre of an anticyclone – the opposite of a trough.

Rime Ice deposits in the form of tiny, white, granular icy feathers, which point towards the wind. This occurs when supercooled cloud or fog droplets come into contact with an object and freeze immediately.

Roll cloud A relatively rare, low-level horizontal, tube-shaped accessory cloud completely detached from the cumulonimbus base. When present, it is located along the gust front and most frequently observed on the leading edge of a line of thunderstorms. The roll cloud will appear to be slowly 'rolling' about its horizontal axis. The most frequent and famous roll cloud is the 'morning glory' cloud in Queensland, Australia.

Rossby waves A series of troughs and ridges in major belts of upper tropospheric westerlies. The waves are thousands of kilometres long and have significant latitudinal amplitude.

Rotor cloud A turbulent cloud formation found in the lee of some mountain barriers when winds cross the barrier at high speed. The air in the cloud rotates around an axis parallel to the range.

S

Saffir-Simpson hurricane wind scale A scale, numbered from one to five where 5 is the most severe, which denotes a hurricane's intensity, determined by the maximum sustained wind speeds. The scale provides examples of the type of damage and impacts associated with winds of the indicated intensity. In general, damage rises by about a factor of four for every category increase.

Samoon A hot swirling wind in the Sahara and Arabian desert that plays a role in reshaping dunes. From the Arabic for 'poison'.

Sandstorm A storm in which sand is carried aloft, 3-4½ m (10-15 ft) above the ground, by strong winds.

Santa Ana wind A strong, hot, dust-bearing wind that descends to the Pacific coast around Los Angeles from inland desert regions.

Sastrugi Ridges of snow formed by the action of the wind.

Saturation The point at which a certain volume of air contains the maximum amount of water vapour possible at a given temperature. If any more vapour is added, or if the air is cooled, condensation occurs.

Scattered clouds When more than 2 oktas and less than 5 oktas of the sky is covered in cloud.

Scattering The process in which the path of a beam of light is altered by interaction with particles suspended in the atmosphere.

Scud clouds Small, ragged, low stratus cloud fragments that are unattached to a larger cloud base. They are often seen behind cold fronts and thunderstorm gust fronts and are generally associated with cool moist air.

▼ *Stinging, invasive sand being blown across a street in a sandstorm in Bandar Mahshahr, Iran.*

Sea breeze Also known as an onshore breeze, a sea breeze is a wind that blows onto the land from the sea. The land heats up more quickly than the sea, resulting in a pressure difference that generates thermal circulation.

Sea fog Common advection fog caused by transport of moist air over a cold body of water.

Sea ice Ice that commonly forms on the surface of the oceans around the Arctic and Antarctic, reaching peak coverage in the winter, before shrinking back during the summer.

Sea level pressure The atmospheric pressure at sea level at a given location. When observed at a reporting station that is not at sea level, a correction applied to reflect the pressure as though the station is at sea level.

Sea smoke Also known as 'steam fog', 'frost smoke', 'warm water fog' and (quite wonderfully) 'the barber'. This occurs when cold air moves over water around 10°C warmer, causing water to evaporate at a higher rate than the air can absorb. The excess water vapour rises upwards towards drier air, giving the impression of steam or smoke. It occurs most frequently in areas of open water surrounded

▶ *Sea smoke rising from the relatively warm water of Suomenlinna, Helsinki, Finland.*

by sea ice, but can also be seen over lakes and rivers, especially in autumn when water bodies are still warm after the summer.

Sea surface temperature The mean temperature of the ocean in the upper few metres.

Seasons Away from the tropics, there are four seasons in a year – Spring, Summer, Autumn and Winter. In meteorology, these are defined using three calendar month blocks, and

astronomically by the solstices and equinoxes. The different seasons are caused by the 23.5° inclination of the Earth's rotational axis in relation to the plane around which it orbits the sun. This means that over the course of a year, certain parts of the globe are tilted towards the sun, while other areas are tilted away from it, resulting in a change in the amount of light and heat we receive, leading to changes in the weather. The tropics

are warm all year, as the tilt has much less of an effect and there is more exposure to the sun. Most of the tropics will see a wet season, but the amount and duration of rainfall varies markedly.

Secondary pollutant Pollution generated by chemical reactions in the atmosphere.

Seeder-feeder mechanism Theory proposed by Bergeron in 1949, describing how precipitation falling from an upper level cloud (seeder) falls through a lower level (feeder) cloud capping a hill or mountain, collecting moisture and producing greater precipitation than on nearby flat land.

Sensible heat flux The transfer of heat from the Earth's surface to the atmosphere that is not associated with phase changes of water. It is an important component of Earth's surface energy budget.

Sheet ice Ice formed by the freezing of liquid precipitation or the freezing of melted solid precipitation.

Sheet lightning The most common type of lightning. Clouds are illuminated by a lightning discharge, but the lightning channel is either inside the clouds or below the horizon, so is not visible to the observer.

Shelf cloud A low, horizontal, wedge-shaped arcus cloud,

attached to the base of another cloud and usually associated with a thunderstorm (or occasionally with a cold front). Shelf clouds usually form along the leading edge of a storm and are outflow features associated with cool air. The underside of a shelf cloud appears turbulent and they are often mistaken for wall clouds.

Shipping forecast A weather forecast specifically designed to cover conditions over open water, concentrating on wind and sea states, issued by numerous maritime nations, and a crucial part of safety at sea.

Shortwave solar radiation Radiant energy emitted by the sun at and around the wavelength of visible light, between about 0.1 and 2 micrometres.

Shower Precipitation falling from cumuliform cloud that is intermittent in time, space or intensity and is characterized by the suddenness with which it starts and stops.

Single cell thunderstorm A type of thunderstorm that develops in weak vertical wind shear environments. It is characterized by a single updraft core and a single downdraft that descends into the same area as the updraft, which cuts off the thunderstorm inflow and causes the updraft and the thunderstorm to dissipate. Single cell thunderstorms are short-lived – they only last about half an hour to an hour – but occasionally become severe, producing large hail, strong wind gusts or tornados.

Sirocco A hot south or southeasterly wind which blows from the Arabian or Sahara deserts offshore across the sea, when low pressure cells move east across the Mediterranean, causing dusty dry conditions along the north coast of Africa, storms in the Mediterranean and cool wet weather in southern Europe. It may last up to several days, with wind speeds up to 100 kmh, mainly in autumn and spring.

Sleet Mixed rain and snow, or snow that is melting as it lands. In North America, the word

has a different definition, used to denote ice pellets – a totally different phenomenon.

Slush Snow or ice on the ground that has been turned into a soft watery mixture by rain and/or rising temperatures.

Smog A type of air pollution, named using a portmanteau word that combines 'smoke' and 'fog'. Classic smog results from the build-up of airborne pollutants at ground level – mostly arising from the burning of coal – which act as catalysts for fog, as water clings to the tiny particles. In the 1950s a new type of smog – photochemical smog – was described, formed by the interaction of pollutants and sunlight. It usually restricts visibility and can be hazardous to health.

Snow Precipitation in the form of ice crystals, joined together in a complex hexagonal pattern to form snowflakes. Snow appears white because it reflects the sunlight equally at all wavelengths. Snow grains are usually less than 1 mm in diameter, while snow pellets are about 2 to 5 mm in diameter.

Snow drifts Deep areas of snow which occur when the wind blows snow into big piles.

Snow flurries Slight snow showers which are usually intermittent and of short duration with no measurable accumulation.

◄ *Shelf cloud on the leading edge of an incoming thunderstorm in Minnesota, USA.*

Snow roll A rare meteorological phenomenon, also known as 'snow rollers', 'snow donuts', 'snow bales' and 'wind snowballs', in which the wind causes the top layer of snow to produce a variety of shapes.

Snow stick A portable rod used to measure snow depth.

Snowline The vertical limit of snow lying on a mountain side throughout the year.

Solarimeter A device used to measure the amount of solar radiation reaching a given surface.

Solar radiation The total electromagnectic radiation emitted by the sun, providing varying amounts of heat at different latitudes and at different times of the year, driving Earth's weather and climate patterns.

Solstice The time when the sun is at its most northerly or southerly excursion relative to the celestial equator. The summer solstice occurs around 21st June in the northern hemisphere, and around 22nd December in the southern hemisphere when the sun reaches its northern or southernmost point on the celestial sphere. The dates of the winter solstice when it reaches its opposite point are reversed. These events lie halfway between the equinoxes and, astronomically speaking, mark the beginning of summer and winter.

SNOW

For those of us poleward of latitude 40° there is the chance every winter of waking up in the morning to a transformed world, where gardens, roofs and roads have been covered by nature's best attempt at a whitewash. Welcomed by those wanting to build a snowman, go skiing or sledging, snow can be a wonderful sight, but too much of it and it can become life threatening.

Snow forms when temperatures are low and the moisture making up **cloud**s is in the form of small ice crystals. These tiny crystals stick together as they move around in the cloud, becoming snowflakes. When they become heavy enough they fall from the cloud. If the air below the cloud is between 0° and 2°C (32° and 35.6°F) they tend to stick to each other and create bigger 'wet' flakes. If they fall through cold, dry air the snow will be powdery and 'dry'.

Amongst snow's stunning natural creations are the rare but beautiful **snow rolls**. Snow rolls look just like rolled up cylindrical hay bales, appear randomly scattered across snow-covered fields and vary in size from tennis balls to as much as 2 m (6½ ft) wide. They don't occur in isolation, there are generally a lot of them, scattered around. For snow rolls to form, the ground needs to be covered by a layer of **ice** or dry powder snow to which snow will not stick. The ice must be covered by wet, loose snow, the temperature of which is close to melting point. The wind also must be strong enough to both start and then keep the snow rolls rolling, but not strong enough for them to collapse or blow apart. If the wind is blowing down a slope, gravity helps in the formation of the snow roll

and they are more common in hilly areas than on the flat. They are often hollow in the middle, where the first layers to form are weak and thin compared to outer layers and can easily be blown away. They are stunning natural sculptures that are so rare most people have never even heard of them, let alone seen one.

However, not all snow brings joy and pleasure. When very cold air is pulled in around a deep low pressure system, precipitation often falls as snow, with many centimetres accumulating on the ground, causing difficulties for many ordinary aspects of life, notably transport systems. If the wind whips up then this can turn into a snowstorm – but not every snowstorm is just a snowstorm. A **blizzard** is a specific type of snowstorm, lasting at least three hours, with winds of at least 50 kmh (30 mph), visibility of less than 400 m (437 yds) and temperatures near the ground and up in the clouds below 0°C (32°F). Usually, it's formed by large amounts of snow falling from clouds, but occasionally a ground blizzard can form, whipping up snow lying on the ground to create similar conditions. Often it's a combination of the two and can be deadly.

Blizzard conditions most often form on the northwest side of a powerful storm in Russia, central and northeast Asia, northern Europe, Canada and the northern United States. In Antarctica they are associated with winds blowing over the edge of the ice plateau at speeds of 160 kmh (100 mph), but blizzards can occur elsewhere, including mountaintops in the tropics.

▶ *Nature's perfect cylindrical snow roll formed on a hillside near Malborough, Wiltshire, England.*

Southern lights The common name for aurora australis (see Aurora).

Space weather Conditions and phenomena that occur above the mesosphere, including in the thermosphere, exosphere, ionosphere and magnetosphere. Cosmic and solar winds, and coronal mass ejections are important examples. Interest in space weather has grown as complex technologies and infrastructures – including satellites and power grids – have been found to be susceptible to damage by solar flares.

Spanish plume A weather pattern in which a plume of low level warm, dry ex-Saharan air passes over the Iberian Peninsula, combines with higher level moisture coming in from the Atlantic, then travels to northwest Europe, giving rise to an increased risk of severe thunderstorms.

Specific humidity The ratio of the mass of water vapour to the total mass of the moist air.

Spring Meteorologically speaking, the name applied in the northern hemisphere to the months March, April and May, and in the southern hemisphere September, October and November. This season is only really relevant outside of the tropics where four distinct climatic seasons occur. Astronomically it is the period between the vernal equinox and the summer solstice.

Spring tide A tide pattern that occurs when the moon is either new or full and closest to the Earth and the tide-producing effects of the sun and moon align. During a spring tide, high tides are higher than average and low tides are lower than the average. Opposite to neap tide.

Squall A strong wind characterized by its sudden onset, in which wind speed increases by at least three levels of the Beaufort scale, the speed rising to F6 or more (or increasing at least 16 knots and sustained at 22 knots or more) and lasting for at least one minute. It is differentiated from a gust by its longer duration. Squalls are often associated with the passage of fronts, particularly cold fronts, or well-defined troughs. A squall line is a line of active thunderstorms, either continuous or with breaks. Other marked changes are often observed, such as a change of wind direction or falling temperatures.

Stability An indication of how easily a parcel of air is lifted – if the air is very stable, it has little or no tendency to rise (accompanied by clear, dry weather), but if the air is very unstable, it may rise on its own once started.

Stable air An atmospheric state with warm air above cold air, such that vertical movement is inhibited. If clouds form they will be shallow, layered clouds such as stratus.

Stable boundary layer A stable stratified layer that forms at the surface and grows upward, usually at night or in winter, as heat is extracted from the atmosphere's base in response to longwave radiative heat loss from the ground. Stable boundary layers can also form when warm air is advected over a cold surface or over melting ice.

Staccato lightning A short duration, cloud-to-ground lightning strike, which often appears as a single very bright flash with considerable branching.

Station pressure The measured air pressure at a given reporting station.

Stationary front A front between warm and cold air masses that is moving very slowly or not at all.

Stevenson Screen A shelter (from rain, snow, high winds, leaves and animals) for meteorological instruments, that provides a standardized environment in which to measure and record temperature, humidity and pressure. It has louvred sides to allow air flow, is painted white to reflect heat and sits at 1.25 m (4 ft) above the ground.

Sting jet The tail end of a cyclone, named for its resemblance to

▶ *Stevenson screen containing official recording instruments for Rothera Research Station, a British Antarctic Survey (BAS) base on the Antarctic Peninsula.*

a scorpion's tail. The winds in a sting jet, which reach in excess of 160 kmh (100 mph), are considered the most damaging and life threatening.

Storm A weather system accompanied by strong winds and often other destructive weather such as heavy rain, thunderstorms and/or hail. In the shipping forecast, storm force winds are defined as either a 10 minute mean wind speed of 89–102 kmh (55–63 mph) or gusts to 112–126 kmh (70–78 mph).

Storm surge An abnormal rise in sea level due to an intense storm moving over a body of water, resulting from strong winds and low atmospheric pressures.

Stratiform Meaning to have extensive horizontal development, as opposed to the more vertical development characteristic of convection. Stratiform clouds cover large areas but show relatively little vertical development. Stratiform precipitation is generally continuous and uniform in intensity.

Stratocumulus One of the ten characteristic cloud types (or cloud genera) recognised by the World Meteorological Organization. Low level, relatively flat layer clouds that sometimes join together but can also form in rows, bands or waves. Often forms on the back side of a cold front, producing slight rain or drizzle. From the Latin for layer and heap.

Stratopause The boundary between the stratosphere and mesosphere.

Stratosphere The part of the atmosphere in which temperature increases with height, extending from the top of the troposphere (approximately 13 km/8 miles) to the base of the mesosphere (approximately 50 km/31 miles).

Stratospheric ozone An ozone shield that prevents excessive ultraviolet radiation from reaching the Earth's surface.

Stratus One of the ten characteristic cloud types (or cloud genera) recognised by the World Meteorological Organization. A grey layer of cloud with a fairly uniform base, which may produce drizzle or slight snow. Its name come from the Latin 'strato', meaning layer.

Striations Grooves or channels in cloud formations, arranged parallel to the flow of air, which provide an indication of the airflow relative to the parent cloud.

Sublimation The transition of a substance from the solid phase directly to the vapour phase, or vice versa, without passing through an intermediate liquid phase. An ice crystal or icicle sublimes under low relative humidity at temperatures below 0°C (32°F).

▶ *Striations running around a cumulonimbus cloud in Imperial, Nebraska, USA.*

Subtropics The areas immediately north and south of the tropics, approximately between 23.5° and 35° latitude, characterized by hot summers and mild winters with little or no frost.

Sudden Stratospheric Warming (SSW) Occasions in the winter when the polar stratosphere rapidly warms and the usual flow of westerly winds in the polar vortex weakens or even reverses, with cold air rapidly descending, affecting the shape of the polar jet stream.

Summer Meteorologically speaking, the name applied in the northern hemisphere to the months June, July and August, and in the southern hemisphere December, January and February. This season is characterized by having the warmest temperatures of the year, and is only really relevant outside of the tropics where four distinct climatic seasons occur. Astronomically this is the period between the summer solstice and the autumnal equinox.

Sun dog Another name for parhelion.

Sun pillar An optical phenomenon produced by ice crystals in cirrus clouds. It is a bright column above or

▶ *Sun dogs either side of the sun on the 22° halo, partial 46° halo, light pillars, upper tangent arc and the parhelic circle seen from the Halley Research Station, Antarctica.*

below the sun, produced by the reflection of sunlight from ice crystals in cirrus clouds.

Sun rays Rays of sunlight that penetrate through holes in clouds as columns of sunlit air, divided by darker shaded regions.

Sunrise The time at which the first part of the sun becomes visible above the horizon in the morning at a given location.

Sunset The time at which the last part of the sun disappears below the horizon in the evening at a given location.

Super typhoon A typhoon with maximum sustained winds of 130 knots (150 mph) or greater.

Supercell thunderstorm Potentially the most dangerous type of convective storm. A thunderstorm cloud is strengthened by a strong continuously-rotating updraft (or a 'mesocyclone') that may exist for several hours. Storms possessing this structure generate the vast majority of long-lived strong and violent tornadoes, as well as downburst damage and large hail.

Supercooled liquid water In the atmosphere, liquid water can survive at temperatures colder than 0°C (32°F). Supercooled liquid water is important in the formation of graupel and hail.

Supersaturation The condition that occurs in the atmosphere

when the relative humidity is greater than 100%.

Surface energy budget The energy or heat budget at the Earth's surface, considered in terms of the energy fluxes (radiative, sensible and latent heat) through a plane at the Earth–atmosphere interface.

Surface weather chart A synoptic chart of surface weather observations, showing the distribution of sea-level pressure (the position of highs, lows, ridges and troughs), the location and nature of fronts and air masses.

Sustained wind The surface wind speeds obtained by averaging observed values, usually over a 10 minute period.

Synoptic scale chart A map showing large-scale weather patterns in an area at a given time.

Synoptic scale systems Features typically with a range of many hundreds of kilometres, including cyclones and anticyclones.

◀ *Well-developed supercell thunderstorm, with a single deep, persistent updraft over Chamberlain, Saskatchewan, Canada.*

T

Tail cloud A horizontal, tail-shaped cloud at low levels (not a funnel cloud), extending from the precipitation region of a supercell toward the wall cloud.

Teleconnection The climate variability links between geographically separated areas. One of the most striking is that linking sea level pressure at Tahiti and Darwin (Australia), which defines the Southern Oscillation.

Temperate Climate in the mid-latitudes characterized by moderate rainfall, sporadic drought, mild to warm summers and cool to cold winters.

Temperature A measure of how hot or cold it is, with reference to a standard value.

Temperature inversion Layer of atmosphere where air temperature increases with height.

Tephigram Thermodynamic diagram used to plot upper air soundings and assess instability, depth of moisture/cloud layers, fog points, temperature of free convection, condensation level.

Thaw A warm spell of weather that causes ice and snow to melt.

Thermal A relatively small-scale, rising air current produced when the Earth's surface is heated – a common source of low level turbulence for aircrafts.

Thermal wind A theoretical wind that blows parallel to thickness lines and relates the magnitude of the horizontal temperature gradient in a defined layer to the real winds that blow at the top and base of that layer. The speed of the thermal wind is proportional to the gradient.

Thermograph An instrument used to measure and record air temperature, producing a trace or image over a period of time.

Thermometer An instrument used for measuring temperature. usually in units of Kelvin (K), Fahrenheit (F) or Celsius (C)

Thermosphere Region of the Earth's atmosphere where temperature increases with height. It begins above the mesosphere, about 80-85 km (50-53 miles) above the Earth, and extends to the exosphere.

Thickness lines Thickness measures the difference in height between two standard pressure levels in the atmosphere. Thickness lines on charts join points with equal thickness, and are an indicator of the temperature of an air mass.

Thunder The sound caused by a flash of lightning and the subsequent intense heating of the air which causes gases to rapidly expand. Temperatures can rise to over 10,000°C in microseconds.

Thundersnow An unusual winter thunderstorm in which snow (or graupel or hail) falls instead of rain. It typically occurs in regions of strong upward motion within the cold sector of an extratropical cyclone.

Thunderstorm A local storm produced by a cumulonimbus cloud, accompanied by lightning and thunder and usually producing gusty winds, turbulence, heavy rain, sometimes hail and, under extreme conditions, tornadoes.

Tipping-bucket rain gauge A device for measuring the amount of precipitation. Collected water is funnelled into a seesaw-like bucket; after a pre-set quantity of rain falls, it will fill one side of the bucket and overbalance the lever so that it tips, emptying, then the other side of the bucket moves into place beneath the funnel. As the bucket is tipped, it activates an electrical circuit to log the 'tip' and record the amount of rainfall has fallen. The advantage of the tipping bucket rain gauge is that the character of the rain (slight, medium or heavy) may be obtained, as well as the quantity.

Tornado A violently rotating column of air stretching from the base of a cumulonimbus or towering cumulus cloud to the ground. It nearly always starts as a funnel cloud and may be accompanied by a loud roaring noise. It can vary considerably in width and have a lifespan ranging from minutes to hours.

On a local scale, it is the most destructive of all atmospheric phenomena. Upon impact with the ground, strong winds associated with a tornado can kick up dust and debris and cause great destruction.

Towering cumulus A large convective cumulus cloud with great vertical development, usually taller than it is wide due to its strong updrafts, but lacking the characteristic anvil of a cumulonimbus.

Trade winds Persistent tropical winds that blow from the subtropical high pressure centres towards the equatorial low. They blow northeasterly in the northern hemisphere and southeasterly in the southern hemisphere.

Triple point A point in the atmosphere where three distinct air masses meet, often the point of origin for a cyclone.

Tropical cyclone A warm-core, non-frontal synoptic-scale cyclone, originating over tropical or subtropical waters with organized deep convection and a closed surface wind circulation about a well-defined centre.

Tropical continental air mass An air mass with its origins over land in the tropics, travelling polewards and crossing very little water, characterized by dry and hot air.

Tropical depression A tropical cyclone in which the maximum one minute sustained surface wind is 61 kmh (38 mph) or less.

Tropical maritime air mass An air mass with its origins in the tropics, travelling polewards over water.

Tropical storm A tropical cyclone in which the maximum one-minute sustained surface wind ranges from 63–117 kmh (39–73 mph) inclusive.

Tropics Areas of the Earth located within a band 23.4° north and south of the equator.

Tropopause The upper boundary of the troposphere. It is characterized by a usually abrupt change from the falling temperatures with height in the troposphere, to near-uniform or rising temperatures in the stratosphere.

Tropopause jet A type of jet stream found near the tropopause. Examples of this type of jet are the subtropical and polar fronts.

Troposphere The lowest layer of the atmosphere, from the Earth's surface up to the tropopause, with an average depth of 14–16 km (9–10 miles) around the equator, 9–12 km (5½–7 miles) in temperate latitudes and well below 9 km much of the time in polar regions. It is characterized by a general decrease of temperature with height, vertical wind motion, appreciable water vapour content, and weather (for example, clouds and rain).

Trough An elongated area of relatively low atmospheric pressure, usually stretching out from the centre of a depression – the opposite of a ridge.

Tule fog Fog created by radiative cooling of the ground and the air just above the surface. Usually occurs on clear and humid nights, when the ground cools quickly. Due to the high humidity, the temperature only needs to drop slightly to reach the dew point. Very low wind speeds allow for a deeper fog layer. Tule fog gets its name from the Tule Valley of California.

Turbulence Atmospheric motion that shows irregular and random motion over very small distances and short intervals of time.

Turkey tower Slang for a narrow, individual cloud tower that develops and falls apart rapidly.

Twilight The time just before sunrise and just after sunset when the sun is not directly visible, but all or part of the sky is visibly bright, caused by the scattering of the sun's rays through the upper atmosphere.

Twister A colloquial term for a tornado.

Typhoon A tropical cyclone in the western North Pacific Ocean in which the maximum one-minute sustained surface wind is 118 kmh (74 mph) or greater. It is known as a hurricane in the eastern and central north Pacific and north Atlantic Ocean, and as a tropical cyclone in the South Pacific and Indian Ocean. It is a name of Chinese origin, meaning 'great wind'.

TROPICAL CYCLONES, HURRICANES AND TYPHOONS

Many people living in coastal areas of the **tropics**, such as the Caribbean islands and the Philippines, are well aware of the annual necessity to prepare for the destructive ways of one of nature's most terrifying forces, the tropical cyclone. Known as a hurricane in the North Atlantic and central and eastern North Pacific, a typhoon over the northwest Pacific and under the generic tropical cyclone name in the South Pacific and Indian Oceans, these giant storms are all formed in the same way and are capable of causing wide-scale destruction and loss of life.

Usually occurring between June and November in the northern hemisphere and November to April in the southern hemisphere, a **low pressure** system that forms over tropical or **sub-tropical** waters can be classified as a tropical cyclone, hurricane or typhoon when it intensifies to the point that the maximum sustained winds reach 120 kmph (74 mph).

To form, a tropical cyclone requires warm ocean water - above 26.5°C (79.7°F) to a depth of 50 m (164 ft). It also requires wind so that air moves across the ocean, allowing some warmer surface water to evaporate and then rise in the air - as it rises it then cools and condenses forming **clouds**. There also needs to be a lack of vertical **wind shear** through the depth of the cloud, so that the cloud can develop in height – this continuing process can form large areas of thunderstorm bearing **cumulonimbus** clouds. The core of rising air results in **low pressure** at the surface, and the **Coriolis** force aids a closed low-level circulation to form, with a spinning column of rising air within the cloud. Whilst the system remains over warm water, it's an on-going process, with the clouds growing taller – at least 15,000 m (50,000 ft) high and 200 km (125 miles) across - and the winds getting stronger, with an eye of clear skies in the centre, often less than 8 km (5 miles) wide. The very strong winds and low pressure can result in a huge mound of water to build up in the eye, and this **storm surge**, along with heavy rain falling from the cumulonimbus clouds will cause the most damage if the storm reaches land.

Hurricane strength may be measured on the Saffir-Simpson Scale, which runs from 1 to 5 and is based on the strength of the maximum sustained winds. 5 is the highest rating and has the greatest potential for destruction. Hurricanes are named from a six-year rotating list, updated and maintained by the World Meteorological Organization, of alternating male and female names. Typhoons are categorized such that they become very strong typhoons, then violent typhoons, and super typhoons – the equivalent of a category 4 hurricane. They have a rotating five-year list, with names chosen by the countries affected and generally referring to animals, flowers and astrological names. What the two do have in common, is that when a hurricane or typhoon has caused significant damage that name will be retired and replaced in the list. Hence there will never be another Hurricane Andrew or Typhoon Haiyan.

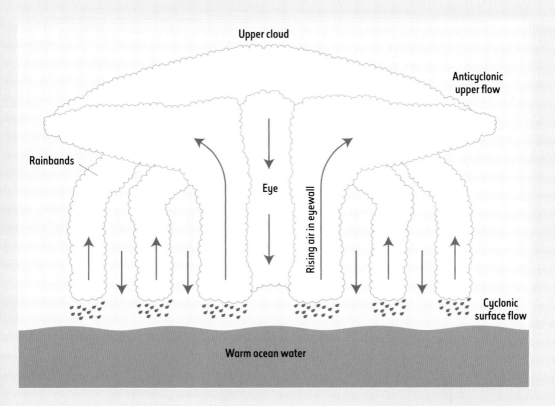

▲ *Tropical cyclones have distinct areas of rising and descending air around a well-defined eye.*

TORNADOES

An iconic image, seen by millions, is the sight of a 'twister' ripping through Kansas at the start of the 1939 film *The Wizard of Oz*. Made from a cone of muslin covered in dirt, connected to a gantry above and a rod in the floor below, it was able to twist and bend as they were moved. The surroundings were made in miniature, and the overall effect was so realistic it inspired many meteorologists to take up their careers, and many storm chasers to want to see the reality for themselves. That reality is one of the most destructive natural weather phenomena on Earth, the tornado.

Tornadoes can last anywhere from several seconds to more than an hour, but most last less than 10 minutes. Typically between 20 to 100 m (60 to 330 ft) wide at ground level, with a track of less than 2 km (1.2 miles) and a wind speed up to 180 kmh (100 mph), the largest can be over 3 km (1.9 miles) wide, have winds of over 480 kmh (300 mph) and track for 100 km (60 miles). By far the highest frequency of tornados is in North America, recording on average 1,200 each year, but they also occur elsewhere, including in northwest Europe, Australia and Bangladesh.

Tornadoes vary in shape, but are most common in the form of a rope tornado. Stronger wedge tornadoes, with a longer track and duration, are mostly larger, more destructive, and can be spotted on radar pictures where a hook shape is formed in the rainfall pattern, with the tornado forming near the point of the hook. The strongest, less than 1% of those recorded, rip buildings from their foundations. **Waterspouts** are the equivalent, less powerful, phenomena formed over the sea.

Most tornadoes are spawned from **thunderstorms** that have a very energetic **updraft**, as warm surface air rushes up into colder air aloft, and where there is strong

vertical shear – the wind direction notably changing in strength and direction with height. This combination sets up a rotating horizontal cylinder of air rising on one side and descending on the other. Changes in **pressure** within this core, and the continued flow of warm and cold air currents can result in this cylinder becoming twisted, confining the rising air to a narrow column. This will

then lower from the cloud base, forming a **funnel cloud** or 'tuba' and, as any rotation in the surrounding descending air magnifies the process, the column will spin faster like an ice dancer pulling in their arms, such that it is at a peak when it reaches the ground. Usually the column will become visible, as water droplets condense within the funnel, often meeting a cloud of rotating dust or debris whipped up

▲ *Tornado, spawned from a cumulonimbus cloud, being watched near Wray, Colorado, USA.*

from the land it crosses. As soon as the vertical column of rotating air, acting like a hoover, reaches the land surface of the Earth it becomes a tornado.

U

Ultraviolet (UV)
Electromagnetic radiation that has a wavelength shorter than visible light and longer than X-rays (between 5–400 nm). Although it accounts for only 4-5% of the total energy of the sun's rays, it is responsible for many complex reactions, such as fluorescence, the formation of ozone and sunburn.

Ultraviolet index A measure of the strength of the ultraviolet (UV) radiation from the sun at a particular place on a particular day (1–2: Low, 3–5: Moderate, 6–7: High, 8–10: Very High, 11+: Extreme). The aim of the index is to warn people of increased risk and encourage them to protect themselves against the risks of skin cancer and skin damage.

Undulatus Clouds that appear in patches, sheets or layers, showing clear undulations. This cloud variety results when the air above the cloud layer and the air below move at quite different velocities.

Unstable air Air that is able to rise easily, and has the potential to produce cumuliform clouds, rain and thunderstorms.

Updraft A small-scale current of rising air. If the air is sufficiently moist, then the moisture condenses and forms a cumulus cloud or an individual tower of a towering cumulus.

Upper air Usually indicates the levels between 850 mb (about 5,000 ft), and 200 mb (39,000 ft).

Upslope fog Fog that forms when moist, stable air is carried up a mountain slope. The air cools adiabatically, and if the temperature of the air drops to the dew point temperature, fog is produced.

▼ *The rolling form of undulatus, seen here in stratocumulus cloud on a flight over the central English Channel, from Jersey to Gatwick, England.*

Urban flooding Flooding caused by a lack of drainage in an urban area. High intensity rainfall can cause flooding when the city sewage system and draining canals do not have the necessary capacity to drain away the amounts of rain that are falling.

Urban heat island An urban or metropolitan area that records significantly higher temperatures than those in surrounding rural areas. Its causes include the use of non-reflective heat-absorbing materials (for example, tarmac and concrete); the heat generating effects of industry, transport and air conditioning; urban pollution causing a local greenhouse effect; and a relative lack of vegetation to absorb heat and carbon dioxide from the atmosphere.

Vapour pressure The partial pressure of water vapour in the atmosphere.

Veering winds Winds that shift in a clockwise direction at a given location (for example, from southerly to westerly), or else change direction in a clockwise sense with height (for example, southeasterly at the surface, southwesterly aloft).

Vernal equinox The equinox that occurs in Spring.

Virga Precipitation that falls from a cloud, but evaporates or sublimates before reaching the Earth.

Virtual potential temperature The temperature a parcel of air at a specific pressure level and virtual temperature would have if it were lowered or raised to 1,000mb. This is defined by Poisson's equation.

Virtual temperature The temperature that a parcel of air containing no moisture would need to have to equal the density of a parcel at a specific temperature and humidity.

Visibility The greatest distance toward the horizon at which a prominent object can be seen and identified with the naked eye.

Visible light The segment of the electromagnetic spectrum, with wavelengths between 380 and 700 nanometers, that the human eye can detect.

Volcanic ash Fine particles of mineral matter from a volcanic eruption that can be dispersed long distances by upper level winds. If it is blown into the stratosphere and it is thick enough, it can decrease the global temperature. Such particles can seriously affect aircraft and machinery on the ground.

Vortex A whirling column or spiral of air. It need not be oriented vertically but, for example, could be rotating around a horizontal axis.

Vorticity A measure of the rotation of air in a horizontal plane. Positive (cyclonic or anti-clockwise in the northern hemisphere, clockwise in the southern hemisphere) vorticity is associated with surface low development and upward vertical motion.

VIRGA

It is not unusual to be out and about when the sky starts to darken, and you look up to see dark, rain-bearing clouds heading ominously in your direction; you then pull on a waterproof or pop up an umbrella. The wind picks up, the temperature drops, the clouds roll overhead - but nothing happens; the clouds pass and the sky clears, leaving you to pack up the waterproof, fold down the umbrella and wonder if you'll bother with them next time. But next time you may well get wet, this time what's just passed over you is known as virga.

Virga is, very simply, an observable streak of **precipitation** – be that **rain**, **snow** or **ice** - that falls from a **cloud** but doesn't reach the ground, meaning that nothing below it actually gets wet. It can be seen not just from threatening **nimbostratus** or **cumulonimbus** clouds, but also trailing from **cirrocumulus**, **altocumulus**, **altostratus**, **stratocumulus** and **cumulus** clouds.

As it falls, precipitation will evaporate or **sublimate** if it passes through a sufficiently thick layer of drier or warmer air. This can be caused by a process called 'compressional heating', which causes air to heat up as the air pressure increases closer to the ground. But it can be a fine balance – the **phase changing** virga will pull heat out of the surrounding air as it descends, making that air denser than its surroundings. This denser air accelerates towards the ground and, in some circumstances, this may create a rapid **downdraft** called a 'dry microburst'. A dry microburst can be extremely dangerous to aviation, especially when it spreads out in hitting the ground causing low-level **wind shear**, hazardous during take-off and landing aeroplanes.

At higher levels fine and wispy virga may result in a striking 'jelly fish' cloud. More commonly, streamers of falling water are caught by wind shear underneath the cloud, with the tail forming a hooked shape. Both of these can produce dramatic and beautiful scenes, especially when lit by a red sunset. Surprisingly, the occurrence of virga is not confined to Earth - sulphuric acid that rains out of the sky on Venus boils away before it reaches a surface which is hot enough to melt lead.

▶ *Distinctive jellyfish-like trails of virga, formed by rain falling from altocumulus cloud but evaporating high above the observer, at Point Sublime on the North Rim of the Grand Canyon, California, USA.*

W

Wake The region of turbulence immediately to the rear of a solid object caused by the flow of air over or around the object.

Walker circulation A large scale cell comprising east to west atmospheric circulation along the equatorial belt, induced by the contrast between the warm waters of the western Pacific and the cooler waters of the eastern Pacific

Wall cloud A localized, persistent, often abrupt lowering from a rain-free base. Wall clouds can range in diameter from a fraction of a mile to nearly 8 km (5 miles), and are usually found on the south or southwest (inflow) side of the thunderstorm. When seen from within several miles, many (but not all) wall clouds exhibit rapid upward motion and cyclonic rotation. Rotating wall clouds usually develop before strong or violent tornadoes.

Warm front The boundary between a mass of advancing warm air and the colder air it is replacing. Generally, with the passage of a warm front, the temperature and humidity increase, the pressure rises, and the wind shifts. Precipitation, in the form of rain, snow or drizzle, is generally found ahead of the surface front. Fog is also

common in the cold air ahead of the front.

Warm sector A region of warm surface air between a cold front and a warm front.

Water cycle Also known as the hydrological cycle, the water cycle describes the movement of water on, above or below the surface of the Earth. The mass of water on Earth remains fairly constant over time but the partitioning of the water into the major reservoirs of ice,

fresh water, saline water and atmospheric water depends on a wide range of climatic variables. The water moves from one reservoir (river, ocean, land, atmosphere) to another by the physical processes (evaporation, condensation, precipitation, infiltration, surface runoff, subsurface flow) and in doing so, the water goes through different forms (liquid, solid, gas).

Water vapour Water in its gaseous form.

Waterspout Usually starts as a funnel cloud that gradually stretches down to sea level, resulting in a small, rotating column of air running between the cloud and the surface of the sea. Most common over tropical or subtropical waters, and less violent than its land based equivalent, the tornado.

▼ *Rotating columns of air called waterspouts stretching from cumulonimbus clouds down to the sea off Mali Losinj, Croatia.*

Wave In the atmosphere a wave is formed when the air undergoes a series of disturbances that are regular and organized, resulting in energy being moved from one place to another in an organized pattern.

Wavelength In the atmosphere the distance between two equivalent points on adjacent waves e.g. two adjacent troughs.

Weather The state of the atmosphere (for example, sunny or cloudy, dry or wet, calm or windy, cold or warm) at a specific time and place.

Weather bomb Also known as a 'bomb cyclone', this is a colloquial term for a low pressure system with a central pressure that falls very rapidly (24 millibars in 24 hours) in a process known as explosive cyclogenesis, which can produce violent winds.

Weather forecast A prediction designed to provide information on the likely weather today and a few days ahead. Meteorologists produce forecasts using observations, computer models and their knowledge of the atmosphere and local topography.

Weather satellite A type of satellite used to monitor the atmosphere, weather and climate of Earth. These can be polar orbiting (covering the entire planet) or geostationary (hovering above the same point on the equator). Using specialist equipment, they collect information about, for example, clouds, pollution, forest fires, volcanic ash, auroras, dust storms, snow, ice and ocean currents.

Weather station A set of observing equipment used to collect and record information about the weather (for example, temperature, humidity, precipitation, pressure, wind speed and direction, solar radiation).

Weather vane An often decorative instrument that indicates the wind direction.

Westerlies The prevailing winds that blow from the west in the mid-latitudes.

Wet bulb thermometer Used to measure the lowest temperature in the ambient atmosphere in its natural state by evaporating water from the wet muslin-covered bulb of a thermometer. The wet bulb temperature is used to compute dew point and relative humidity. It is one of the two thermometers that make up a psychrometer.

Wet microburst A microburst accompanied by heavy precipitation at the surface.

Whirlwind A small, rotating column of air. May be visible as a dust devil.

Wildfire Any uncontainable wildland fire that consumes the natural fuels and spreads in response to its environment.

Williwaw A type of katabatic wind characterized by a sudden blast of cold, dense air descending from a mountainous coast to the sea, primarily used in the Strait of Magellan, the Aleutian Islands and Alaskan fjords.

Willy-willy A term given to a dust devil in Australia. Also formerly used to denote a tropical cyclone.

Wind The motion of the air relative to the surface of the Earth. It is caused by variations in temperature and pressure (for instance, air rises as it warms and a cool breeze moves in to take the place of the rising air). There are four areas of wind that are measured: direction, speed, character (gusts and squalls) and shifts. Surface winds are measured by wind vanes and anemometers, while upper-level winds are detected through pilot balloons, radiosonde or aircraft reports.

Wind chill The additional cooling effect resulting from wind blowing on bare skin, based on the rate of heat loss from exposed skin caused by the combined effects of wind and cold. In short, it is the temperature the body 'feels'.

Wind direction The direction that the wind is blowing from (for example, southerly wind is blowing from the south). It can be expressed in cardinal directions (one of the 16 points of the compass) or from 0° to 360° (for example, north is 360° or 0°, and south is 180°).

Wind shear The change in wind direction, speed, or both, either in a vertical or horizontal plane. Vertical wind sheer is the change in the wind's direction and speed with height and is important in the study of convection, particularly for severe storm development. Horizontal shear is the change in wind speed and direction with distance.

Wind speed The rate at which the air is moving past a given point at a given time. It may be a ten-minute average speed (reported as wind speed) or an instantaneous speed (reported as a peak wind speed, wind gust, or squall). It is usually described in units of miles per hour (mph), metres per second (m/s), knots (kn) or Beaufort force.

Wind vane An instrument used for showing the direction of the wind, usually as an architectural ornament on the highest part of a building.

Winter Meteorologically speaking, the name applied in the northern hemisphere to the months December, January and February, and in the southern hemisphere May, June and July. This season is characterized by having the lowest temperatures of the year, it is only really relevant outside of the tropics where four distinct climatic seasons occur. Astronomically it is the period between the winter solstice and the vernal equinox.

Wintry showers Term used to describe showers producing soft hail, sleet or snow when the air temperature is close to 0°C.

▼ *Wildfire spreading through the Chita region, Russia.*

X

Xerothermic climate A climate that is both hot and dry. Derived from the Greek word xeros, meaning dry.

Xlokk The Sirocco wind in southeast Malta (pronounced 'shlock').

X-ray Electromagnetic radiation with wavelengths between 0.01 and 10 nanometers or between gamma rays and ultraviolet radiation. All X-rays from space are absorbed in the Earth's upper atmosphere.

Y

Yalca A severe snowstorm that occurs in the Andes Mountains in northern Peru, characterized by a strong squally wind.

Yamase A cool onshore breeze, bringing days of low cloud, rain and fog to the Senriku district of Japan.

Yellow snow Snow with a golden or yellow appearance usually caused by the presence of pine or pollen.

Youg A hot wind during an unsettled summer in the Mediterranean.

Z

Zephyr A westerly warm and gentle breeze, originally at the time of the summer solstice in the northern hemisphere.

Zonal flow Large scale atmospheric flow in which the latitudinal component is dominant. Opposite of meridional flow.

Zonda A Fohn wind that blows eastwards over the Andes in Argentina.

Zulu time One of several names for the 24-hour time used throughout the scientific, aviation, maritime and military communities as well as by those working in meteorology. Other names include Universal Time Coordinate (UTC) or Greenwich Mean Time (GMT).

-90 -80 -70 -60 -50 -40 -30   -20   -10   0   10   20   30   40 | C°

▲ *An infrared image taken from a geostationary satellite, looking down on Typhoon Yutu, taken on 24th October 2018 over northern Mariana Islands and Guam in the Pacific Ocean. The weather satellite detects heat energy (regardless of the time of day or night) in the infrared spectrum (invisible to the human eye) and displays images based on the temperature of the closest surface to the satellite. The range of colours indicate the range temperature of the cloud tops, in this image the darker blues are registering temperatures of around -50°C (-58°F) and the yellow around -80°C (-112°F).*

PICTURE CREDITS

ACKNOWLEDGEMENTS

Editor and author: Adrienne Le Maistre
Section author: Gavin Pretor Pinney
Section author: Viel Richardson
Original concept development: LSC Publishing

First published by the Natural History Museum,
Cromwell Road, London SW7 5BD

© The Trustees of the Natural History Museum,
London, 2022

ISBN 978 0 565 09529 1

A catalogue record for this book is available
from the British Library

10 9 8 7 6 5 4 3 2 1

Designed by Bobby Birchall, Bobby&Co
Reproduction by Saxon Digital Services
Printed by Toppan Leefung Printing Limited, China